PBH
D1833174

THE ECONOMY OF INDIA

THE ECONOMY OF INDIA

Global Challenge for the Century

Jean-Joseph Boillot

GYAN PUBLISHING HOUSE
New Delhi–110002

The Economy of India: Global Challenge for the Century

Rs. 360

© Jean - Joseph Boillot

ISBN : 81-212-0948-X

All rights Reserved. No Part of this book may be reproduced in any manner without written permission.

Published in 2008 in India by
Gyan Pulishing House,
5, Ansari Road
Darya Ganj, New Delhi-110002,
Phones: 23282060, 23281060,
Fax: 23285914
Email: books@gyanbooks.com.

Lasertype Setting by: Tact Computer Graphics, Delhi
Printed at: Vishal Kaushik Printers, Delhi

Contents

Contents

List of Tables

FOREWORD

The Indian economy is poised to become one of the biggest economies of the world. We now, on the one hand, have one of the largest numbers of millionaires and billionaires. On the other hand, we still have millions of poor and hungry people. The disparity is also evident between urban and rural standard of living and between regions and states. Our young professionals have acquired international competitiveness in cutting edge technologies and services. On the other hand, agriculture, which provides livelihood to more than half the population is still languishing in backwardness and stagnation.

This book written by a foreign scholar gives a very balanced view of the Indian growth dynamics. It traces the evolution of the Indian economy, going back to thousand years, in identifying the cycles of growth and standard of living. He has taken a detached view of the contradicting schools of thought on the Indian economy. Though, more sympathetic to the market oriented reform, he also stresses the constraints and compulsions arising from backwardness in agriculture, and regional disparities. The beauty of the book lies in its precise narration of the developments in the pre and post reform period. In this respect, this could be a very useful text book for the graduate and post graduate students on the Indian economy.

B.B. Bhattacharya
Vice-Chancellor
Jawaharlal Nehru University
New Delhi-110067

INTRODUCTION

The Indian economy is a picture of contrasts: on one side, there is mass poverty and, on the other, the development of centres of excellence in the services industry. These two realities coexist within the same economy, an economy of continental proportions now in a process of complete transformation. Measured in purchasing power parity (PPP), India clearly ranks fourth worldwide as regards its GDP, or fifth if the European Union is considered as a single entity. Its population crossed the one billion mark in 2000 and is likely to exceed China's population between 2025 and 2030, stabilizing itself at about 2 billion by the end of the 21st century. India, which had isolated itself from the world economy after its independence, was forced to accelerate the pace of its new development strategy adopted in the 1980s after the balance of payments crisis in 1991. Will the acceleration of its rate of growth to more than 6% per year and a more offensive stance on globalization translate into the emergence of a new economic superpower alongside China? Although less centred on the export of manufacturing platforms, India's take-off has occurred during a crucial phase of the globalization of the services industry in which this country has a clear-cut advantage thanks to the presence a large pool of qualified manpower and competitive centres recognized by global firms. This book will attempt to answer this question by analysing the internal and external challenges faced by the world's largest democracy.

On the domestic front, India's slow but undeniable awakening is marked by a twofold challenge: a democratic political system (650 million registered voters in 2004) and mass poverty (27 per cent of the population) which question the logic of development economics on the link between democracy and economic take-off and the risk of dualism that has affected so many developing countries in the past. The works of the Indian Nobel laureate, Amartya Sen, provide a typically Indian theoretical synthesis suggesting a combination of four intellectual traditions that India could preserve in the years to come: a conservative frugal Gandhism still alive notably in the Indian NGOs; a social-democratic Nehruism still present within the Congress party; a more traditional kind of social-communism still in force in Bengal and in Kerala; and lastly the devotion to "Lakshmi" (the Indian goddess of prosperity) deeply embedded in the traditional business communities which inspires Indian capitalism deeply imbued with the spirit of liberalism which has been growing rapidly since the first reforms were introduced in the 1980s.

On the external front, the rising economic power of India following China with a lag of 10 to 20 years is certainly not irreversible, but the growing probability of this happening has revived the debate on the future of the world economy in the 21st century with the emergence of two new giants aspiring to the status of superpower alongside the United States and eventually Europe. What place and what role is India prepared to assume in this new geoeconomy? What challenge does it represent for all of us in terms of environmental sustainability? What are the adjustments required of historic industrial powers now in a state of demographic decline?

The book starts with some historical indicators, including well corroborated ones, to demonstrate that the Indian economy is not a newcomer on the world stage and that its historic decline from the 17th century largely explains the self-reliant model it chose to follow after Independence in 1947. Chapter II concentrates on the gradual breakaway from this model after the failure of the Emergency in 1977 and the coming into power of Indira Gandhi's son, Rajiv.

It will be followed by the major turnabout in 1991 that sought to dismantle the "License Raj" blamed for the famous "Hindu Rate of Growth" of barely 1 per cent per capita growth during the first three decades after Independence.

In the second part, the book concentrates on the internal structure of the Indian economy (Chapter III) starting with the essential factor of the demographic transition and its socio-demographic dynamic to examine the development in the fields of agriculture where India occupies the fourth place in the world, the low speed of industrialisation as opposed to the revolution in the services sector which seems relatively atypical of this level of development. This part concludes with a discussion on a theme which is central today: why growth does not reduce poverty more quickly in India?

In the third part, the book discusses the external challenges faced by India, firstly in the current situation of globalization and redefinition of the post-cold-war world economy. Globally, India remains a marginal trading partner but the extension of the service offshore paradigm to the industrial sector translates into a strong dynamic of opening up a country that has now adopted an offensive stance in the international arena (Chapter V). Lastly, Chapter VI tries to project India's position in the world economy during the period 2025-2050, perhaps a futile exercise for such a long span of time but quite useful to measure the demographic, economic, environmental and geopolitical impact of the reborn India.

1

India's First Steps Towards a Modern Economy

1.1. From Prosperity to Colonisation by the British

To understand modern India, it is necessary to go back into her past for two reasons. The first relates to the long history of the world economy which includes phases of contraction and expansion of large parts of the world. In this regard, the historical works of the economist Angus Maddison [2003], even though imperfect, paint a correct picture of India in the 1700s when it was one of the world's leading economies together with China, each of them accounting for almost 23 per cent of the world GDP. So what would be more natural than for these two giants to finally return to an economic position commensurate with their demographic importance, India's present population amounting to almost 20 per cent of the world's population?

The second reason is more subjective and relates to the mechanisms of a relative decline observed in the 18th century as a result of which India's economic position dropped to approximately 16 per cent of the world GDP in 1820, while a swift decline in the 19th century brought it down to a historical low of 3.8 per cent during the 1950s. The term *subjective* indicates in particular the perception widely prevalent in India that external causes, particularly colonization by the British, were responsible for its decline. This perception is also the source of a major trait of its development policies based on the idea of *self-reliance*, the leitmotiv of the post-independence period which continued till the end of the 1980s and whose vestiges are still visible in the present collective mind-set. It is also subjective because India's present bounce-back and its renewed confidence have been inspired by its pride in its five thousand-year civilization which has known several glorious eras in the past.

The Arthashastra and a Prosperous India

The first myth about India is that it was an underdeveloped economy at the time of its independence. The *Arthashastra*, which could be roughly translated today as a "Treaty on Good Governance" is attributed to Kautilya, adviser to the great king Chandragupta Maurya who ruled around 321-290 B.C. It shows a rare understanding of the importance and the means of a prosperous economy: "acquired wealth should not be hoarded, it should be spent (...) the path of moral rectitude is unceasing work for the acquisition of wealth and profits." A good king is one who imposes reasonable taxes, develops infrastructure and encourages trade as well as farming. As a matter of fact there were several prosperous kingdoms in Indian history when dynamic merchant castes expanded India's sea-trade to Southeast Asia and the Middle East along what is popularly known as the *Spice Route,* with dynamic trading centres like Malacca, mid-way on the route to China. The same is true of the land route, the famous *Silk Route*, one of whose branches crossed present-day Pakistan to reach Gujarat (Surat) and brought great wealth to the famous Jain and Marwari merchants.

In later centuries, this prosperous India described by Deleury [1991] in his book "*Indes florissantes*" went through difficult times due to a change in the political circumstances. The Indian subcontinent was in a constant state of upheaval as Muslim invaders from Central Asia first attacked the coastal areas in the south and later the northern plains. During the 14th and 15th centuries, the Indian subcontinent was fragmented between the sultanates of the north and the kingdoms of the Deccan. In the south in particular, early Portuguese sailors were deeply impressed by the splendour of the capital city of the Hindu kingdom of Vijayanagar, which fell in 1565, and the magnificence of its army. The kingdoms of the Malabar Coast witnessed the rise of merchants who made vast fortunes by trading in spices, especially pepper and ginger which abound in the areas of Eli and Calicut, in the Indian Ocean. On the east coast, under the Gajapati (master of elephants) dynasty, Orissa, which is today one of India's poorest states, rose to the height of its glory between 1435 and 1568 thanks to the cultivation of rice in the Mahanadi delta, sugar-cane and spices and, finally, the recovery of salt from its coastal swamps. Even its textile industry, though it could not compete with those of Gujarat and neighbouring Bengal, underwent an unprecedented growth with the production of luxury fabrics combining fine white cotton and silk yarn. And that brings us to the legendary Golconda diamond, the biggest in the world, found in the mines of the Golconda Sultanate, established by an Azerbaijani named Quli Qutb-ul-mulk (1512-1543), which proclaimed its independence in 1512 and dominated the Asian diamond market for several decades. It was this India that attracted new-comers – Arab traders followed by Europeans, with the Portuguese coming in 1498 and the other European trading companies between 1565 and 1600: the Dutch VOC was established in 1594, the East India Company was launched in London in 1600 and the French East India Company was set up by Colbert in 1664 after the failure of smaller companies as far back as 1528 (when the ship *Marie du bon secours* ran aground off Diu).

The Mogul Empire (1556-1739) is a part of this glorious phase in spite of the continual military campaigns in the subcontinent and a significant change in the economic structure. At the beginning of Akbar's reign in 1556, India had a population of 100 to 145 million of which 60 per cent came under direct Mogul rule. It was then the largest population in the world of which 15 to 20 per cent lived in urban areas. The vast majority of the population, which was Hindu and rural, was subjected to heavy taxation and did not benefit from any technical innovation that could raise the agricultural output. On the other hand, the volume of trade increased rapidly due to the unprecedented fascination of Europeans for Indian textiles produced in workshops where labour was five to ten times cheaper than in England, and sold by prosperous merchants belonging to the trading castes.

During this time India had a substantial trade surplus and the Mogul rulers amassed sufficient wealth to build splendid monuments for which they are admired to this day. The Taj Mahal, whose construction was started in 1632 by Emperor Shah Jahan (1628-1658) in memory of his wife, Mumtaz Mahal, laid the foundations of the famous Mogul style of architecture which dominated the sub-continent till the 18th century. At the beginning of this century, the Mogul rulers did not allow any political or religious interference even though the first military clashes with the colonisers had started as early as 1687 in Bengal. India's economic prosperity, increasingly shared by European traders who led a fairly modest lifestyle and observed a strict code of behaviour, generated huge profits as well as increased revenue from taxes and customs duties leading to an unprecedented boom in the textile industry and full employment making India one of the leading economic powers in the world.

However, the data provided by Maddison show that during the same period Europe experienced a more vigorous growth due to the first fruits of the agricultural and industrial revolutions accompanied by an explosion of its population which rose by 74 per cent between 1700 and 1820 as against only 37 per cent in India. Above all, its per capita GDP was certainly much higher than India's, which remained stagnant, the ratio being 2:1 in 1820. What was only a relative decline actually corresponded to a profound change in the balance of power in the world. Undermined from within and incapable of changing its political and socio-economic structures, the Mogul Empire, which had remained essentially agricultural, disappeared within three decades of Aurangzeb's death in 1707. India then witnessed a mushrooming of sultanates and kingdoms that were still prosperous but incapable of attaining political stability, so much so that the new European powers, and later just England, established themselves as the new masters imposing a colonial model which would finally end in India's underdevelopment when the British Raj came to an end in 1947.P.

Percentage of World GDP

Years	INDIA	CHINA	JAPAN	Rest of ASIA	W EUROPE	USA	L. AMERICA	AFRICA	OTHERS	WORLD (Billion $ ppp 1990)
1	33	26	1	16	11	0	2	7	4	103
1000	29	23	3	16	9	0	4	12	5	117
1500	24	25	3	13	18	0	3	8	6	248
1600	22	29	3	11	20	0	1	7	6	331
1700	24	22	4	11	22	0	2	7	8	371
1820	16	33	3	8	23	2	2	4	9	695
1870	12	17	2	7	33	9	2	4	13	1113
1913	7	9	3	6	35	19	4	3	16	2732
1950	4	5	3	7	26	27	8	4	16	5330
1973	3	5	8	9	26	22	9	3	16	16024
2001	5	12	7	13	20	21	8	3	9	37194

Percentage of World GDP Population

Years	INDIA	CHINA	JAPAN	Rest of ASIA	W EUROPE	USA	L. AMERICA	AFRICA	OTHERS	Million hab
1	32	26	1	16	11	0	2	7	4	230820
1000	28	22	3	15	9	0	4	12	5	267573
1500	25	23	4	13	13	0	4	11	7	438428
1600	24	29	3	12	13	0	2	10	7	556148
1700	27	23	4	12	13	0	2	10	8	603490
1820	20	37	3	9	13	1	2	7	9	1041834
1870	20	28	3	9	15	3	3	7	12	1271915
1913	17	24	3	10	15	5	5	7	14	1791091

1950	14	22	3	16	12	6	7	9	12	2524324
1973	15	23	3	17	9	5	8	10	10	3916489
2001	17	21	2	20	6	5	9	13	8	6149006
Percentage of 100=World Average Per Capita GDP									calcul	USDppp 1990
1	101	101	90	101	101	0	90	97	97	445
100	103	103	97	103	92	0	92	97	100	436
1500	97	106	88	100	136	71	74	73	87	566
1600	92	101	87	95	149	67	74	71	92	595
1700	89	98	93	92	162	86	86	68	98	615
1820	80	90	100	87	180	188	104	63	103	667
1870	61	61	84	73	224	279	78	57	113	875
1913	44	36	91	58	227	347	97	42	114	1525
1950	29	21	91	43	217	453	119	42	142	2111
1973	21	21	279	50	279	408	110	34	158	4091
2001	32	59	342	66	318	462	96	25	116	6049

Source: MADDISON A. [2003], The World Economy, Historical Statistics, OECD, Paris.

British Colonisation and its Consequences

British India went through two distinct phases. The first century under foreign rule (1757-1858) was dominated by the East India Company. India's conquest began with the defeat of Nawab Siraj-ud-daula at Plassey (Bengal) and ended in 1858 with the abolition of the Company's monopoly. India came under the direct rule of the British Crown after the defeat of the Marathas in 1818 and then the quelling of the Sepoy Mutiny in 1857 which created a complete political vacuum in the sub-continent. Between 1765 and 1858, there were twelve terrible famines which became a distinctive feature of colonial India. Agricultural stagnation accompanied by a rapid population growth was further aggravated by the instability of the government as the new rulers were more interested in exporting India's commercial wealth [Lafont, 2005].

The second colonial century (1858-1947) began with the expansion of the British rule over the entire sub-continent and ended with India's partition in 1947 leaving behind a country whose GDP was barely 4 per cent of the world GDP while its population amounted to 14 per cent of the world population. As for agriculture, the first phase extending up to World War I witnessed the coexistence of a rise in prices with an expansion of the area under cultivation and of the transport and irrigation networks. But despite this development, there were twenty famines with the one in 1860 causing two million deaths, while those in 1865 and 1876 in South India are estimated to have killed between 10 to 20 per cent of the population and put an end to the development of the southern part of the sub-continent and, finally, the famine of 1896 which caused more than five million deaths. The second period, which lasted till India's independence, was characterised by insufficient agricultural output due to the increase in population growth and low prices of agricultural products. But paradoxically, there were no famines during this period due to improved preventive measures. However, the last big famine in India, the Bengal famine of 1943, caused almost four million deaths and left a profound impression on the Indian Nobel laureate, economist Amartya Sen, who was then a young student.

Historians feel that the performance of the colonisers in the field of agriculture left much to be desired: "In spite of the visible economic success in some favoured areas and among a few strata of the Indian farming community, the general state of India's agricultural underdevelopment was taking its present shape and was responsible for its slow and unequal growth." [Markovits, 1994] Further, the decline of the Indian economy under British colonisation hinged on a triple mechanism elucidated by the Indian economists Datt and Sundharam [2004]: the decline of village industries and the progressive ruralisation of the Indian economy, the introduction of a new landowning system and the shift towards the cultivation of cash crops for purposes of export and, finally, a pattern of industrialisation subordinated to the interests of metropolitan areas and subjected to the vagaries of the global situation marked by the Great Depression of the 1930s. As regards the last point, the performance of colonial powers is far from ambiguous. While rural crafts and cottage industries were destroyed by competition from large industries developed initially by the British, notably as a part of the Managing Agency system, Indian trading communities like the Parsis, Gujarati Baniyas, Marwaris, Jains and Chettiars, began to amass huge amounts of capital and acquire greater technical expertise which enabled them to gradually to gain the upper hand in the economic field over the colonisers. It is estimated that they controlled 70 per cent of the Indian economy on the eve of independence as against the 30% dominated by foreign capital. It was they who supported the nationalist Swadeshi movement (India for Indians) of 1905 that sought to adapt production to domestic demand. It was also they who imposed selective protective measures on the domestic industry – especially steel, textiles, jute, sugar and paper – to the point of gradually driving out foreign producers. The theory that underdevelopment was incontestably the result of colonisation was disputed by some economists like Morris D. Morris [1982] who shed more light on the peculiarities of wage formation in the early stages of Indian capitalism.

1.2. The Foundations of India's Development Policy: 1947-1980

India gained its independence in August 1947 in a climate of grave political and economic instability which lasted till the adoption of a republican constitution in 1950. Severe communal riots tore the country apart at the time of its partition from Pakistan, which itself was divided into two parts – the western part, which is Pakistan as it exists today, and the eastern part which broke away in 1972 to form what is now Bangladesh. Millions of people left their homes, the majority in the two parts of Punjab and Bengal. In 1948, the assassination of Mahatma Gandhi by a Hindu fanatic belonging to the RSS, and the death of the founder of Pakistan, Mohammed Ali Jinnah, were followed by the first armed conflict over Kashmir where a cease-fire was declared only in 1949. Within the country, the annexation of Kashmir and Hyderabad illustrates how difficult it was to unify the country, not taking into account the last colonial outposts, among them Pondicherry which officially joined the Indian Union only in May 1956 after its actual transfer in 1954. The economic situation was then catastrophic with recurring food shortages together with the shortage of essential raw materials like jute and cotton, and finally an uncontrollable inflation. This critical situation would leave a strong imprint on the first Indian economic model whose influence is still perceptible. However, as compared to the Chinese model, the Indian post-independence model was less radical. It owed its origin to at least four different influences which were dominant in different periods, namely Nehruism essentially inspired by social democracy, Soviet and later Chinese communism and today its Indian version, the more or less moderate liberalism of the trading classes and, finally, Gandhism.

Box – Chapter 1 – The Four Sources of India's Economic Thought

- The first modern economic ideas made their appearance in 1938 with the setting up of a National Planning Committee under the leadership of Jawaharlal Nehru, one of the main figures of the

Indian independence movement. Inspired by Fabian socialism during his long stay in Great Britain, Nehru also admired the success of the then prevalent Soviet model. The Congress functioned in a political system that claimed to be democratic while pursuing the goal of setting up a socialistic society; its economic ideology thus bore the imprint of the social-democratic tradition coupled with the Third World ideals of the time which laid stress on heavy industry and import substitution. State economic measures assumed the form of an indicative plan that was nonetheless compulsory for the public sector treated as a key sector to determine the country's main political and social preferences. At the same time, in case of a shortage of resources, the state would not hesitate to adopt a series of regulations to control the private sector in order to attain the plan's goals.

- Another trend situated to the far left of the Nehruvian ideology led to the birth of the Communist Party of India in 1925 (CPI). Although it supported the nationalist movement, the Communist Party had a strong identity based on Soviet orthodoxy before its split in 1964 leading to the creation of a pro-Chinese faction calling itself CPI (M). It held that economic planning was absolutely necessary, that it should more extensive and encourage the expansion of the public sector. At the time of Independence, the then world famous revolutionary leader, M. N. Roy, brought out his own *People's Plan*. This trend remained quite active as the two Communist Parties together were powerful enough to become indispensable partners in a coalition government at the centre.
- The third line of thinking appeared in the *Plan of Economic Development*, popularly known as the *Bombay Plan*, prepared by eight leading industrialists including J.R.D. Tata who headed the largest industrial group in the country. These industrialists supported India's economic independence and considered their plan as a tool to ensure coherence between the ambitious goals of the private sector and

sectors that called for state action, notably infrastructure. It was only after the adoption of the 1956 plan that the Indian industrialists raised their voice against economic planning, particularly through the *Forum of Free Enterprise* set up in 1957. Over the years, the liberal economic ideology gradually assumed importance among the two main political parties that dominate national politics, the Congress and the BJP. But it can be said that only the latter clearly went back to the deep roots of Indian liberalism expressed so explicitly by P.K. Varma and Gurcharan Das.

- Gandhian economic concepts were embodied in the plan formulated by Shriman Narayan and Acharya S. N. Agarwala in 1944. This plan contained a development strategy and a view of social organisation far removed from Nehru's. The Gandhian view was not opposed to the existence of a dominant public sector. Quite the contrary, it was in favour of the state taking over the responsibility of developing key sectors like power and steel. But the four pillars of the Gandhian plan involved reducing the scope and the controlling role of the planned public sector and advocated instead frugality, non-violence, sanctity of human labour (particularly the refusal to replace it with machines) and, finally, humanistic values opposed to the concept of *homo economicus*. Though these ideas may smack of economic romanticism, they had a profound influence on economic thinking during the decades following Independence with the birth of a significant movement of cooperative organisations and NGOs that are still alive and influential.

The "Commanding Heights" Occupied by the Public Sector

The first phase of India's reconstruction that lasted till 1980 was dominated by two principal currents. After the first Five-year Plan (1950-55), which was mainly an exercise in crisis management, the socialist model adopted by India remained dominant till the mid-1980s and owed its origin to the work done by a group of Marxist economists led by P.C. Mahalabonis. His first two-sector model created in 1953 was a simple adaptation of Feldman's Soviet model developed during the 1920s. The Indianisation of the model for the Second Five-year Plan in 1955 simply divided it into four sectors to reflect the importance of services and cottage industries which provided employment to the vast majority of the active population. His macro-economic reasoning gave priority to centralised industrial investment which was meant to determine the maximum long-term rates of saving and growth. The PCM model enjoyed Nehru's complete support and led to the establishment of a mixed economy whose commanding heights were controlled by the state through a dominant public sector and a set of regulations exercising strict control over the private sector, which gave it the disparaging nickname of *Licence Raj* commonly used even today.

Introduced by Nehru in 1950 through the establishment of the famous Planning Commission, economic planning played a decisive role in structuring India's economy from 1955 onwards. At the strictly quantitative level, the share of planned expenditure in the GDP tripled between 1951 and the mid-1970s to go beyond 20 per cent. Above all, it would gradually represent two-thirds of the country's investments and, later, even three-fourths in the Sixth Five-year Plan (1980-85). As far as the central government was concerned, plan expenditure represented 60 per cent of its budget in the early 1980s to which were added another 15 per cent for repaying the interest on the national debt, thus amounting to three-fourths of the total budget.

The public sector is the second part of the socialistic Indian model. The huge *organized* private sector became progressively marginal as compared to the public sector which was given priority in all respects. Within a span of thirty years, its share of the national income (including the administrative setup) rose from 7.5 to 20-25 per cent of which the productive public sector alone accounted for 3 to almost 15 per cent. If we take only the organized sector into account (enterprises employing more than 10 persons), we find that within a few years there was a complete reversal of the public-private sector ratio. Of the 12 million jobs available in 1960, the public sector, which was almost non-existent in 1950, already accounted for 7 million. This figure soared to 21 million in 1970 as compared to barely 7 million in the private sector. Sector-wise, the dominant character of the public sector was even more evident as it represented 84 per cent of the organized sector in 1979 in mining, 88.5 per cent in power, 100 per cent in transport and 81 per cent in communications. As for banks, the figure rose from 12 per cent at the time of independence to 41 per cent in 1965 and then 81 per cent in 1980 after the wave of nationalisation unleashed by Indira Gandhi. Finally, even though agriculture and the manufacturing industry escaped domination by the state, they were subjected to indirect controls in the form of policies regulating prices and the supply of inputs in the case of the former and the industrial policy in the case of the latter. As regards the *organized* manufacturing industries, the share of the public sector rose by several percentage points in the 1950s to more than 10 per cent in 1960 and reached almost 25 per cent in 1979. But having been extended to all types of industries (including the unorganized sector), the public sector no longer occupied the *commanding heights* of the Indian economy as, at the peak of 1980, it accounted for only 14.4 per cent of he total GDP of the country's manufacturing industry. The major decisions taken in the 1940s as a part of the industrial and trade policies constituted the third important part of mixed economic model adopted by India by giving the government considerable means of control.

Date	Major Political and Economic Events in Modern India
1489-1517	Sikandar Lodi, an Afghan, is the Sultan of Delhi
1510	Conquest of Goa by the Portuguese
1556-1605	Rule of Mogul Emperor Akbar
1600	Establishment of the British East India Company in London

1628-1658	Rule of the more liberal Mogul Emperor, Shah Jahan (builder of the Taj Mahal)
1658-1707	Shah Jahan's austere son Aurangzeb, the last great Mogul Emperor, seizes power
1664	Colbert launches the French Compagnie des Indes Orientales
1757-1858	British win the battle of Plassey and the first colonial century
1818	Annexion by the East India Company of the Peshwa's territory
1857	The Sepoy Rebellion. First Indian universities set up
1858-1947	Second colonial century: abolition of the East India Company; India brought under the direct rule of the British Crown after Queen Victoria's procla-mation.
1947	Independance of India and Pakistan.
1948	Assasination of Gandhi and death of Jinnah. Kashmir and Hyderabad join India. First Indo-Pak war over Kashmir.
1950	Launch of the Planning Commission under J. Nehru's chairmanship
1951	First Five-year Plan and general elections.
1956	Second Five-year Plan with a socialistic orientation.
1962	Sino-Indian war on India's northern borders.
1964	Death of Nehru. Lal Bahadur Shastri takes over. Split of the Indian Communist Party.
1965	Second war with Pakistan, LOC established in Kashmir.
1966	Indira Gandhi, J. Nehru's daughter becomes Prime Minister. Deep economic crisis: drought and 36 per cent depreciation of the Indian rupee.
1969	Nationalisation of commercial banks.
1970	Adoption of the Monopolies and Restrictive Trade Practices Act (MRTP) which exercises

	a strict control over the large-scale private sector.
1971	Third war with Pakistan and independance of East Pakistan which becomes Bangladesh. 5th general election and reelection of Indira Gandhi.
1973	The Foreign Exchange Regulation Act (FERA) exercising a strict control over flow of capital and foreign investors.
1975-1977	Proclamation of Emergency by Indira Gandhi and radicalisation of politics.
1977	End of the Emergency. Morarji Desai (Janata party) becomes Prime Minister.
1980	Congress (I) returns to power following Indira Gandhi's reelection with an overwhelming majority. She adopts a more pragmatic economic approach towards private business.
1984	Assassination of Indira Gandhi, her son Rajiv becomes Prime Minister and speeds up economic liberalisation.
1989-91	A non-congress coalition wins the election but proves to be quite unstable in a difficult international situation.
1991-96	Rajiv Gandhi assassinated during the election campaign. The Congress returns to power. Drastic fall of foreign exchange reserves provokes a financial crisis. Launch of the first generation of liberal reforms by Finance Minister, Manmohan Singh.
1997-98	Several coalitions try to take over from the Congress including the BJP which becomes a leading national party within a few years.
1998	Second nuclear test at Pokhran. The international community imposes serious sanctions against India and Pakistan at a time when the world economy is badly shaken by the Asian financial crisis.

1999-2004	The new NDA coalition led by the BJP wins the 13th general elections. For the first time in Indian history, a coalition governement completes its 5-year term. Economic reforms continue but at a slow pace. Political tension caused by BJP's Hindutva ideology lead to major communal disturbances, particularly near the Ayodhya temple and in Gujarat where several thousand Muslims are killed in 2002.
2004	The Congress-led UPA coalition wins the general election with the support of left parties. The new Prime Minister, Manmohan Singh, adopts a pragmatic approach under the slogan "reforms with a human face" which replaces the BJP's "India Shining" campaign. Second generation economic reforms are implemented gradually despite opposition from the left parties. To get their support, special social programmes like the National Employment Guarantee Act and the Right to Information Act are implemented.

The "Licence Raj"

In view of the severe resources crunch, the *Industrial Policy Resolution* of 1948 (IPR) defined the domains reserved for the public sector, the private sector consisting large industries and the small-scale industries sector (SSI). Indian industry was divided into four main sectors, two of which were a state monopoly both at the centre and in the states, while the third was predominantly public and covered a wide variety of civilian industries and the fourth, described as the *reminder of the industrial field*, was totally under the private sector. For the first time, the IRP stipulated the state's right to nationalise any enterprise in the name of public interest. Finally, as far as foreign investment was concerned, the post-independence Indian economic model exhibited a striking trait that is visible to this day: "It is quite normal that major interests related to the ownership of capital and the effective control of management should be in the hands of Indians."

This resolution was followed in 1956 by a second IPR containing a new classification of industries covered by the public and private sectors. To counterbalance the more liberal regime adopted for the large-scale private sector, it defined for the first time quotas and industries reserved under the small-scale sector (SSI, Village and Cottage Industries). In addition, regional priorities which would have a profound impact on India's economic geography also found mention, especially remote districts in states like Madhya Pradesh, Rajasthan and the area that is now Jharkhand.

The new resolution of December 1977, adopted during the short reign of the Janata Party, accentuated the distortions favouring small industries and maintained the predominant role of the public sector on the grounds that the large-scale private and foreign enterprises had failed to create sufficient employment opportunities. The number of products reserved for SME jumped from 180 to 807 and the cooperative and cottage industry sectors, e.g. Khadi in the textile sector as a tribute to Gandhian ideals, received greater support at all levels. Each of these laws was accompanied by regulations introducing domestic licences to limit the production capacity of every enterprise and fixing quotas in the realm of foreign trade. The principal document was the Industrial Development and Regulation Act adopted for the first time in 1951. It laid down the conditions for obtaining industrial licences as well as the lower limit below which a licence was not required (100 employees or equipment worth less than Rs.1 million in the 1950s). Following severe criticism of the perverse effects of the *Licence Raj*, a new Industrial Licensing Policy was adopted in February 1970, but it further complicated the rules for issuing licences despite a more precise definition of what represented a *core sector* predominantly under government control.

The almost obsessive desire to limit the expansion of large Indian companies and foreign firms reached its peak with the adoption in the 1970s of two important laws, the Monopolies and Restrictive Trade Practices Act (MRTP) and the Foreign Exchange Regulation Act (FERA), which would put them under the discretionary control of the Reserve Bank of India and the Ministry of Finance until 1993.

Table 1.2. 55 Years of Planning in India: Main Performance Indicators

	GDP growth: annual average		*Per capita GDP*	*Financing %*		
	Target	*Achieved*		*Budget*	*External support*	*Borrowings*
1st Plan (1951-56)	2.1	3.7	1.8	73	10	17
2nd Plan (1956-61)	4.5	4.2	2.0	56	24	20
3rd Plan (1961-66)	5.6	2.8	0.2	59	28	13
3 annual plans (1966-69)	5.5	3.9	1.5			
4th Plan (1969-74)	5.7	3.4	1.0	74	13	13
5th Plan (1974-79)	4.4	5.0	2.7	82	15	3
Annual Plan (1979-80)	5.0	-5.0	-8.3			
6th Plan (1980-85)	5.2	5.5	3.2	78	8	14
7th Plan (1985-90)	5.0	5.8	3.6	75	9	16
2 annual Plans (1990-92)	5.5	3.3	0.9			
8th Plan (1992-97)	5.6	6.8	4.6	86	5	9
9th Plan (1997-02)	6.5	5.6	3.6			
10th Plan (2002-07)*	8.0	6.5*	4.8*			

Source: Datt [2004] and Economic Survey 2004-2005, Government of India.

* First three years.

The "Hindu Rate of Growth"

As a result of the distressing experience during the first three decades, India's post-independence economic model was questioned in the 1980s. The economic results, which belied the initial hopes and were popularly described as the "Hindu rate of growth", peaked at an annual increase of 3.5 per cent of the GDP, a per capita growth barely +1 per cent. Later India would face a multitude of political and economic crises which would progressively undermine the legitimacy of the original model. Two main phases can be distinguished during this period: the Nehruvian era from 1950 to 1964, followed by a radical change in 1965 ending in the deplorable state of emergency that lasted from 1975 to 1977. The appraisal of the results of 55 years of planning or the appraisal of India's performance in the sub-phases in the next chapter is unambiguous. India's per capita GDP rose by about 1 per cent per annum between 1950 and 1980 and the gap between the goals set by different plans and their results continued to increase after the initial phase marked by a sustained effort to build up the economy during the first two Five-year Plans. India experienced a series of food shortages and payments crises due to the failure of the monsoon, as for example in 1965, which jeopardized the coherence of the plans and particularly the investment effort. Consequently, the latter decreased during the second phase of this period with an annual growth of 4.5 per cent of which only 3.7 per cent went towards investment in machinery and capital goods. Besides, the abrupt change of policy giving priority to agriculture and agro-industries put in jeopardy the initial efforts undertaken in the capital goods sector where the import-substitution model, still very much in vogue in the Third World, made the "self-reliance" model totally responsible for its success [Boillot, 1985]. Though there were tangible results in the form of self-sufficiency in the agricultural sector, the oil crisis in 1974 threw the Indian economy into disarray while the political situation worsened during the second half of the 1970s with the declaration of the state of emergency and the end of Indira Gandhi's rule in 1977. To resolve the problem, an intensive debate took place between renowned economists such as K.N. Raj [1984], one of those who coined the expression "Hindu rate of growth", and the early reformers among whom was Ashok Desaï, joined later by Isher Judge Ahluwalia [1991], wife of the man who would later become the principal economic adviser of Manmohan Singh, father of the economic reforms of 1991.

2

India's Economic Reforms: 1980-2005

The return to power of Indira Gandhi's Congress (I) in 1980 was accompanied in the early stages by the same populist rhetoric advocating state-control. The new Sixth Five-year Plan (1980-85) was inspired to a large extent by the guiding principles of the preceding plan and the electoral campaign of 1981 and centred around the same slogans of *Garibi Hatao* (banish poverty) and "self-reliance". However, the Indian economy would undergo a gradual but profound change as far as its political configuration, its economic strategy and its performance were concerned. With an average growth rate of about 6 per cent, the per capita income more than doubled (from 1.4 per cent to 3.6 per cent) and economists began to talk of the take-off of the Indian economy. It is worthwhile to point out that this rise coincided with the changes in China (following Mao's death in 1978) even though the changed development strategies of the two countries followed a fundamentally different logic. At the political level, the era of reforms ushered in by Deng Xiaoping was a radical process launched from the top by the same authoritarian regime. In India, the new political configuration indicated the failure of the trend towards authoritarianism and the "commanding heights" of the government which admitted its weakness vis-à-vis various interest groups. The democratic system prospered, but not without a profound change in the electoral sociology which would henceforth be dominated by caste-based vote-banks [Jaffrelot, 2005b] and the emergence of regional parties which would compel all-India parties to accept coalitions, even though fragile, at the centre. The Indian reform process thus corresponded more to a movement from the bottom toward the top and its democratic nature, though far from perfect, was in tune with its gradual advancement, its inclination towards consensus and effective performance that, in the short run, was not as impressive as China's.

2.1. The Hindu Rate of Reform in the 1980s

The new balance of payments crisis in 1980 triggered by the second oil crisis forced Indira Gandhi, who had just made a triumphal comeback, to approach the IMF then headed by the Frenchman Jacques de Larosière. Despite the Americans who were obsessed by India's close ties with the Soviet Union, India had no difficulty in obtaining a loan of 5 billion SDRs. But this loan was subjected to such stringent conditions that it gave rise to fervent demonstrations in the country. Measures for relaxing internal and external regulations, though accepted, were nevertheless implemented in a selective manner and on a case-by-case basis, which gave rise to the expression "Hindu rate of reform" reflecting the legendary inertia of India's bureaucracy and its political parties. Thus the industrial license regime was gradually relaxed, especially after Rajiv Gandhi, Indira's elder son, came to power in early 1985 after his mother's assassination in 1984. In the same year, companies whose assets were below Rs.50 million were almost totally exempted from licenses. Similarly, large industrial groups subjected to the tyranny of the MRTP Act were granted licenses automatically if the amount involved was under Rs.1 billion, a measure which gradually led to competition in the domestic market. The system of import and export licenses was also progressively liberalised to encourage industrial modernisation and exports were given priority to ease external pressures. Finally, the tax structure was rationalised and tax rates, which had reached an absurd level (more than 100 per cent of accrued taxes on income from assets), were lowered. However, all said and done, the old system of controls continued and customs duties were actually increased to compensate for the lowering of non-tariff barriers.

Table 2.1. Macro-Economic Growth Parameters during the Four Economic Periods (1950-2001)

	Phase I (1951-52 to 1979-80) subperiod			*Phase II (1980-81 to 2001-02) subperiod*		
		I A	*I B*		*II A*	*II B*
	Phase I	*(1951 -64)*	*(1965 -79)*	*Phase II*	*(1980 -91)*	*(1992 -2001)*
Growth rate (%)						
GDP (market prices)	3.6%	4.4%	2.9%	5.7%	5.5%	6.0%
Per capita GDP at market prices	1.4%	2.3%	0.6%	3.6%	3.3%	3.9%
Private consumption (PFCE)	3.2%	3.7%	2.8%	4.7%	4.5%	4.9%
Government consumption (GFCE)	5.8%	6.6%	5.1%	6.3%	6.0%	6.6%
Investment (GDCF)	6.1%	7.9%	4.5%	6.3%	5.0%	7.8%
Machinery & equipment	6.6%	9.7%	3.7%	8.9%	9.9%	7.9%
Private GFCF	3.6%	3.5%	3.8%	8.5%	8.4%	8.6%
Goods and Services Export	3.8%	0.0%	10.2%	9.5%	8.4%	10.8%
Oil Import			37.1%	9.8%	6.9%	13.2%

Sources: CSO (Series at 1993-94 prices); RBI (Series converted using implicit price deflator for GDP).

Notes: Data about GDP available till 2002–03 and about other aggregates available till 2001–02.

The New Pro-business Stance

Actually, according to serious econometric studies [Rodrik & Subramanian, 2004a], it was not so much the reforms or a more favourable external environment or even the effects of the green revolution that explained the change in India's performance, but a dynamic change in the pattern of growth due to a change in the government's attitude towards the private sector. In a situation where India was still very far from its production goals, these small changes triggered a strong and rapid response in the form of improved productivity, which accounts for more than half the gains of the takeoff during this period. The manufacturing machinery set up gradually since 1950 would be the main beneficiary of the new environment. The inauguration in 1984 of the joint-venture between the Japanese automobile company Suzuki and the Indian public-sector enterprise Maruti set up by Indira Gandhi's younger son, Sanjay, was the first symbol of India's new industrial age. Even today, Maruti-Suzuki accounts for more than half the private cars sold in India and Suzuki is now the dominant partner in the joint venture.

The economic performances of this decade of gradual change are significant. The per capita economic growth rose from 3.3 per cent to 5.5 per cent. Private consumption increased at an unprecedented pace (+4.5 per cent) while investments, which had dipped to a historical low of +5 per cent per annum, increased and swerved in a totally new direction favouring the private sector (+8.4 per cent) and production of capital goods (+9.9 per cent). The rapid growth of exports (+8.4per cent) made it possible to considerably relax the restrictions on the import of more efficient modern machinery and open up the contry to the electronic revolution which was in full swing in the world. The important contract signed with Alcatel in the mid-1980s was another important symbol for a country having one of the lowest telephone densities in the world where a subscriber had to wait for ten years to get a new telephone connection. The total productivity of the various production factors became positive rising from -0.4 per cent par annum in the 1970s to +2.5 per cent per annum during the 1980s. Finally, it is certain that agriculture benefited from the fruits of the green revolution with an annual growth of 4.2 per cent and a contribution of 21 per cent to the rise of the GDP during this decade. The normally capricious monsoon was relatively stable during this period, but what was really responsible for this change was the resilience of the economy as a whole thanks to the dynamism of the services and manufacturing sectors and the increased resilience of the agricultural sector following the introduction of new varieties of seeds, the progress of irrigation and the public distribution system which made it possible to adopt a more active pricing policy favourable to the average farmer.

An Incomplete Transformation: The Crisis of 1991

Considering the progress made by India during the previous decade, what brought about the balance of payments crisis in 1991 when its foreign exchange reserves dipped so low that they were barely sufficient for two weeks and the international situation, especially the oil situation, was very tense as a result of the first Iraq war? Contrary to all appearances, the foreign exchange crisis was only the tip of the iceberg for India's public debt had soared during the 1980s. The accumulation of budgetary deficits was an overt sign of an incomplete transformation. On the one hand, the Sixth and Seventh Five-year Plans (1985-90) had tried to uphold the active role of the public sector through everincreasing subsidies while the tax revenue was falling due to a greater dependence on pressure groups. The gross debt which amounted to 46 per cent of the GDP in 1982 rose to 63 per cent in 1987-88 and crossed 75 per cent in 1990. With debt servicing charges increasing by 22 per cent per annum between 1979 and 1987, economists [Boillot, 1992] expected things to reach a critical point around 1990-92. The external debt kept rising due to the growing need for public finances which continued to absorb all the private domestic savings. This explains why the private sector's external borrowings increased during this period which saw the emergence of a new type of private debt: deposits by non-resident Indians (NRIs) who were attracted by a law enacted in 1983 in order to reduce the pressure exerted by international organisations. In 1988, India became the biggest debtor in Asia with a debt amounting to almost US$60 billion, most of it short-term, and its foreign exchange reserves were in such a precarious state that the country was incapable of facing the oil crisis of 1990. The first phase of reforms had to encounter a double obstacle since India's accelerated growth was not compatible with its budgetary situation that was becoming more and more uncontrollable while its partial trade liberalisation contained too many distortions. It is in these two domains that real reforms were undertaken from 1991.

2.2. The First Generation of Reforms: 1991-2004

The second decade of India's new development model, which started with foreign exchange reserves of less than one billion dollars, crossed the figure of US$ 125 billion by 2004. Its average annual growth rose to 6 per cent and per capita growth to about 4 per cent and for four years it hovered around the 7 per cent desired by Indian planners. The period ended with a growth rate of 8.5 per cent, a fact capitalised by the Hindu nationalist party BJP in its "India Shining" campaign during the general elections of 2004. Nevertheless, the BJP-led coalition (NDA) lost the elections due to a barrage of criticism regarding the unequal distribution of the fruits of growth and its inability to implement what were called secondgeneration reforms and were believed to be indispensable for satisfying the demands of the young people arriving in ever-increasing numbers in the employment market. Interestingly, the initial impetus given to reforms in 1991 lasted no more than a hundred days and this period was characterised by the instability of the political situation, since no party commanded enough support in Parliament to be able to govern alone without forming a coalition which was always ready to pander to excessive populist demands. In fact the severity of the balance of payments crisis in 1991 and the triple shame of having to pledge its gold reserves to the Bank of England, signing a new stand-by agreement with IMF (for 1.8 billion SDR) and, finally, being degraded to the level of Junk Bonds by Moody's, gave rise to a consensus among the political elites on the urgent need for reforms that had been widely discussed all through the 1980s.

Dr. Manmohan Singh Gives the Initial Impetus

The break with the past began with the defeat of the Congress under Rajiv Gandhi in the 1989 elections following which his former Finance Minister, V.P. Singh, became the leader of a disparate coalition formed around the Janata Dal that he had just joined. The Iraq war and its numerous consequences (repatriation of Indians from the Gulf, flight of NRI deposits, rising oil prices, etc.) occurred in the midst of a political crisis triggered by the recommendations of the Mandal Commission for reserving jobs for members of "other backward castes" (OBC) in the public sector. However, V.P. Singh's reformist government became a victim of caste rivalries. After Rajiv Gandhi's assassination, general elections held in May 1991 brought the Congress back to power, but without the requisite majority, under the leadership of Narasimha Rao, a politician totally lacking in charisma. The grave economic situation drove him to appoint as his finance minister a well-known economist, who maintained a low profile but was highly respected for his integrity, and entrust him with the task of putting an end to the economic and balance of payments crises and subsequently taking all the necessary measures to restore growth. In a few weeks, Manmohan Singh brought together a "dream team" consisting of outstanding administrators who restored public confidence and implemented the expected reforms without further delay. He brought in almost the same team when he came back to power in 2004, but this time as Prime Minister. Continuity was also maintained by defining these reforms as "reforms with a human face", an expression dear to Narasimha Rao and the slogan adopted by the Congress in its election campaign in 2004.

One of the major steps taken during the first few weeks was the abolition of the *Licence Raj* in most sectors. Indian industrialists now had full freedom to decide where to invest their money. Nevertheless, the opening up of the economy to foreign investment did not make significant progress despite the fact that investments up to 49 per cent in an enterprise did not require special permission and investments above that level were to be decided on a case-by-case basis. This measure triggered a wave of new business deals in sectors like the automobile sector, telecommuni-cations and IT which had begun to attract a lot of interest. Besides, trade liberalisation advanced rapidly with the dismantling of quantitative restrictions and a sharp fall in customs duties. On the other hand, the rupee was devalued by 30 per cent in 1991 and again by 15 per cent in March 1992. In the public sector, the control over public enterprises was tightened and the government started thinking of privatising and downsizing them, while on the budgetary level, there was a close scrutiny of subsidies in order to put an end to the drain on the national budget. The Planning Commission saw its role being relegated to that an advisory body following a drastic reduction of its financial powers.

First Generation Reforms Lose their Momentum under the NDA-BJP Government

When general elections were held in 1996, the Indian economy had risen from its ashes and seemed, for the first time, to be one of the most dynamic economies in the world after a growth of more than 7 per cent for four consecutive years (1994-97). India was saved from the contagion of the severe Asian crisis of 1997 to a large extent because the markets believed that its fundamentals were solid and its trade and financial structure was not closely integrated with East Asia's. However, the competing devaluation of their currencies by Southeast Asian countries and South Korea forced India to devaluate the rupee slightly in 1997 in circumstances where changes in the domestic cycle of 1993-1997 and the international cycle (the bursting of the dotcom bubble) coincided with a series of poor monsoons. The pace of growth during the second part of the reforms decade slowed down, but at the same time there was a wide consensus in the country about their success with the result that no coalition government could question the direction of the reforms launched in 1991. The pace slackened nonetheless due to party politics whereby when a party joins the opposition, it does everything in its power to obstruct the coalition government in power. The political situation was aggravated by the profound ideological debate between secularism defended by the Congress and Hindu fundamentalism, which is the BJP's hobby-horse. The latter grew in strength from election to election by capturing anti-Muslim (the Ayodhya crisis and the Gujarat riots) and anti-Pakistan votes and reached its climax with the Pokhran nuclear test in 1998 and the new conflict with Pakistan in the Kargil region in the spring of 1999. The two warring countries became the object of a collective animosity on the part of the international community which led to a deterioration of India's economic position for several years and undermined its confidence. The political situation between 1996 and 2004 thus led to a set-back in the implementation of reforms. The 1996 elections resulted in a hung parliament and the BJP leader,

Atal Bihari Vajpayee, renounced power after 13 days although he was short of the majority by only one vote. A United Front government under Deve Gowda came to power in 1996. Within a year, Deve Gowda was replaced by I.K. Gujral as Prime Minister. P. Chidambaram was appointed Finance Minister and tried to breathe a new life into the reforms started in 1991, especially with liberal budgetary reforms. The MRTP Act and FERA were almost abolished and a Disinvestment Commission was set up for the first time. But this experiment lasted less than two years. From 1998 to 2004, it was the turn of the NDA coalition government, led by BJP, to pursue the task of economic reforms. FERA was replaced by FEMA which was much more limited in scope, while the MRTP Act was replaced by a Competition Commission. At the budgetary level, FRBM, an important law related to fiscal responsibility was enacted in 2003 in order to bring down the budget deficit to nil by 2008. On the external front, the liberalisation of FDI was extended to new sectors after the brilliant success of the telecommunications sector and the first hesitant steps in the banking sector, while the lowering of customs duties gathered speed in accordance with the Marrakech Agreements. The first privatisations (discreetly called disinvestment in view of strong public opposition) saw the light of day with the birth of symbolic companies like Maruti-Suzuki and the sale of Hotel Centaur and Modern Foods, the latter to the Hindustan Lever group. Finally, the rupee's external convertibility was relaxed enabling investment funds to operate more freely in Indian financial markets.

Table 2.2. External Debt: Evolution of the Main Indicators since 1970

	1970	1980	1990	1995	1996	1997	1998	1999	2000	2001	2002
Debt service / export (%)	31.5	9.8	32.4	27.8	22.2	21.6	20.6	15.3	14.0	11.7	14.9
Foreign exchange reserves (months of import)	2.9	4.5	0.5	3.9	4.0	4.6	5.1	5.4	5.6	7.0	9.5
Short-term/total external debt (%)	3.4	6.1	10.2	5.3	7.2	5.4	4.4	4.0	3.5	3.0	4.4

Source: World Bank 2004

2.3. Evidence of Need for Second Generation Reforms

India's performance during the years 1991-2004 was quite impressive, particularly in terms of growth and structural change. In spite of the change in the business cycle around 1997-98 and poor monsoons between 2000 and 2002, the fact that the pace of growth during the period was a little more than 6 per cent and its variation coefficient was less than half shows that the economic structure was more stable. The opening up of trade led to a growth of 10.8 per cent per annum in the export of goods and services as compared to 8.4 per cent during the previous decade. Foreign exchange reserves continued to mount and crossed the figure of US$ 125 billion in 2004 and the external debt ratio dropped to a very low level (less than 20 per cent of the GDP) in spite of the increasingly rapid rise in oil imports (15.7 per cent per annum as compared to 6.9 per cent). The rate of investment doubled from +3.8 to +7.8 per cent per annum with the continuation of its tilt in favour of the private sector which went up from 52.6 per cent to 67.6 per cent of the total between the two decades. Customs duties, which had reached a maximum of 150 per cent in 1990-901, were brought down to 30 per cent in 2002, 25 per cent in 2003 and 15 per cent in the draft budget for 2005-06. Finally, the two sectors which now drive India's economic development are manufacturing (+6.8 per cent per annum) and commercial services (+7.5 per cent), especially the modern components of the latter like information technology and banking, have reached a double digit growth. At the same time, India is gradually entering the age of mass consumption, especially its middle class, with private consumption rising by about de 5 per cent per annum and contributing almost 65 per cent to its GDP growth.

Although the first generation of reforms brought about a systemic change in the Indian development model, internal constraints together with the perception of a growing Chinese threat brought about a strong consensus on the need for a second generation of reforms. Over a period of twenty years, China's per capita GDP increased by 50 per cent as compared to India's while it was slightly lower in 1980. On the whole, China's GDP is twice as much as India's with a difference of 3 to 4 points in the annual growth rate which has relegated India to a lower category as compared to its neighbour who evidently aspires to attain the status of a superpower. On the domestic level, the new challenge before India is to reach a systematic growth of 8% per annum as envisaged in the Tenth Five-year Plan (2002-07) and considered indispensable for a significant reduction of poverty and the creation of ten million jobs per year for the country's youth. It is no longer a matter of defining general trends, whose principle is already accepted, but of setting up the necessary institutional environment that is still incomplete and generally mediocre, especially at the legislative level but even more at the administrative level [Debroy, 2004].

3

The Structure of Indian Economy

3.1. The Population

India's population crossed the one billion mark in 2000 when world population reached six billion. With slightly more than 16 per cent of the world population concentrated on 2.4 per cent of the earth's habitable surface, India is a country with a very high population density even though its demographic transition is still incomplete as its population is expected to stabilise at about two billion towards the end of this century.

The Demographic Transition

India's population conforms to the general pattern of demographic transition as it reveals five very distinct phases since 1891. During the first phase which lasted till 1921, the population rose from 236 to just 251 million, i.e. at a negligible annual rate of 0.19 per cent. The birth rate was high, about 49.2 live births per 1000 inhabitants between 1911 and 1920, but the death rate was equally high at about 48.6 per cent. The second phase lasting from 1921 to 1951 was marked by a higher population growth of about 1.2 per cent per annum. It was the result of a slight drop in the birth rate, which fell below 40 per cent between 1941 and 1950, and a sharp fall in the death rate which came down to about 27.4 per cent during this decade. During the third phase lasting from 1951 to 1981, there was a natural peak growth of 2.1 per cent per annum adding 322 million inhabitants to a country which had 361 million in 1951. Nevertheless, the birth rate fell to 37.2 per cent between 1971 and 1980, but the death rate plunged to 15 per cent. The fourth phase from 1981 to 2001 witnessed a slight slow-down of population growth which fell to 2.1 per cent during the first decade and then to 1.9 per cent during the second, but the total population increased by 344 million during this period. However, the birth and death rates indicate that the fifth phase, which in now under way, will probably mark the end of the demographic transition during the next thirty years. The birth rate is now below 25 per cent while the death rate has dropped to a very low level of 8per cent. With the fertility rate of about 2.5 children per woman decreasing every year, the birth rate will slow down to about 21.4 per cent between 2011 and 2016. Natural growth could thus fall below 1.4 per cent with a population of 1,264 million in 2016. But this still means an increase of 17 to 18 million inhabitants every year, which will take India's population to 1.5 to1.6 billion in 2050 according to the last UN forecast (2005), and exceed China's population around 2030. The gap between the two will be very significant towards the end of the century with India's population numbering 1.9 to 2 billion as compared to China's 1.2 billion.

Population Policies

Apart from the slowness of the demographic transition, marked social and regional inequalities have forced the Indian government to control population growth; but its approach is very different from that of its Chinese neighbour. India was the world's first country to officially adopt family planning as far back as 1952, but it was only during the Third Five-year Plan (1961-66) that it set itself the goal of stabilizing its population "over a reasonable period". Thus the goal of bringing the birth rate down to 25 per cent by 1973 was fixed and appropriate means were adopted to spread family planning methods by opening an increasing number of centres in remote rural areas. However, the results were disappointing in spite of a combination of methods such as the widespread use of the media, mass distribution of contraceptives and even financial incentives for voluntary sterilisation by both men and women. This failure explains

Indira Gandhi's exasperation which drove her to take advantage of the state of emergency in 1975 and use coercive methods to speed up sterilization, a step that would lead to her massive defeat in 1977. The sterilisations peaked at 8.3 million in 1976-77, falling to 0.95 million in 1977-78 before rising gradually to 2.8 million in 1981 and 4.9 million in 1985-86.

In fact, the rejection of this coercive policy forced the country to ponder on the deep-seated reasons responsible for a slower demographic transition in India than, for example, in East Asia. A comparison of the relevant social indices determining fertility revealed the strong correlation between the education level, malnutrition and the marriage age of women, which can explain the marked contrast between the performance of Kerala and Uttar Pradesh in the realm of family planning. This led the family planning authorities to concentrate on these aspects and they were supported in their endeavours by a growing number of NGOs who tried to adopt a more comprehensive approach to family planning by including in it the fight against poverty and discrimination against women. The proportion of married women in the 15-44 age group declined progressively from 1981 to reach a level of about 70 per cent as compared to 85.75 per cent in 1961 and 80.5 per cent in 1981.

Composition According to Gender and Age

It is necessary to draw attention to two peculiar features of the population's skewed structure. The deterioration of the sex ratio due to the preference for sons was one of the findings of the 1991 census, and even more of the 2001 census, that excited a lot of comment following the discovery that modern prenatal diagnostic techniques were used for aborting female foetuses as much among the poor as among the rich and as much in rural areas as in big cities. The number of girls per 1000 boys thus fell from 972 in 1901 to a low of 927 in 1991 before rising slightly to 933 in 2001. But here again, there are marked regional differences with 1058 girls in Kerala as compared to 874 in Punjab and 898 in U.P. Paradoxically,

Table 3.1. Main Demographic Indicators in India: 1950-2005 and Forecast up to 2050

	Population in Millions (at the end of the Period)	Density	Crude Birth rate (per 1000)	Crude Mortality rate per 1000)	Fertility (children per female)	Child mortality (per 1000 births)	Life Expectancy (years)	Sex Ratio (males per 100 females	Average age (median)
1950-1955	395	120	45.4	25.4	5.97	19.0	38.7	105.9	20.6
1955-1960	442	135	44.8	22.2	5.92	17.3	42.6	106.6	20.4
1960-1965	495	151	42.4	19.8	5.81	15.7	45.5	106.9	20.1
1965-1970	555	169	40.6	17.7	5.69	14.5	48.0	107.1	19.9
1970-1975	621	189	38.4	15.9	5.43	13.2	50.3	107.4	20.0
1975-1980	689	210	34.8	13.9	4.83	12.9	52.9	107.4	20.6
1980-1985	766	233	34.2	12.9	4.48	10.5	54.8	107.0	21.1
1985-1990	849	258	32.4	11.6	4.15	94.5	57.2	106.7	21.7
1990-1995	936	285	30.1	10.4	3.81	84.9	59.5	106.4	22.5
1995-2000	1021	311	27.2	9.4	3.43	76.2	61.5	105.9	23.4
2000-2005	1103	336	24.6	8.8	3.07	67.6	63.1	105.2	24.3
2005-2010	1183	360	22.5	8.3	2.76	59.7	64.9	104.6	25.6
2010-2015	1260	383	20.7	7.9	2.5	52.8	66.7	104.1	27.1
2015-2020	1332	405	18.9	7.6	2.29	46.8	68.5	103.6	28.7
2020-2025	1395	425	17.0	7.6	2.11	41.7	70.0	103.0	30.4
2025-2030	1449	441	15.3	7.6	1.95	37.5	71.4	102.5	32.2
2030-2035	1494	455	14.2	7.8	1.85	33.6	72.7	102.0	33.9
2035-2040	1534	467	13.7	8.2	1.85	30.1	73.8	101.6	35.6
2040-2045	1568	477	13.1	8.6	1.85	27.1	74.9	101.1	37.1
2045-2050	1593	485	12.4	9.1	1.85	24.5	75.9	100.7	38.7

Source: United Nations, Population Division [2005].

this phenomenon is more noticeable in big cities like Delhi where the number of children per family has gone down significantly together with an unprecedented rise in the number of private clinics offering the latest foetal sex-determination techniques. This bias is beginning to create serious problems for the sex ratio in India's metropolises, which is further affected by the influx of predominantly male workers from rural areas in search of employment. This preference for male progeny is undoubtedly related to the persistence of the dowry system, which places a heavy burden on the girl's family and fosters inflation as the country gets richer, and which is the root cause of a number of human tragedies including the murder of young brides widely reported in daily newspapers. Things have reached such a point that the central government decided in 2005 to make it compulsory for its employees to declare the marriage expenses incurred by them.

The distortion of India's population structure on the basis of age is the second major phenomenon having particularly serious medium-term economic consequences even at the world level. According to the pattern of demographic transition, the age pyramid is distorted towards the top by the famous window of demographic opportunity which causes the dependence ratio to fall in favour of an absolute and relative expansion of the active age group (15-59 years) while the relative impact of aging is quite low. The 0-14 age group thus increased from 38.8 per cent of the population in 1911 to a high of 41.4 per cent in 1971 to drop to about 30 per cent during the 2001 census. Inversely, the 15-60 age group dropped from 60.2 per cent to a low of 53.4 per cent to rise again to almost 61 per cent in 2001. The relative aging of the population is thus quite noticeable. The rapid increase of life expectancy from 41.2 years during the 1951-61 decade to almost 65 years in 2004 resulted in an increase of the over-60 group from 1 per cent of the total population to almost 7 per cent between 1911 and 2001. This means that the relative burden of the dependent population is less than 3 per cent in a country where the maximum age of retirement is at best 65 years. In comparison, the relative aging population is three times higher in China than in India which has already taken the first steps towards an ambitious reform of its pension system.

Urbanisation and Migration

The Indian demographic revolution was accompanied by an increasing population density. From 77 persons per square kilometre, the average density rose to 324 in 2001, just a little below Japan's (336). But it is expected to increase by 50 per cent during the next 50 years and stabilise towards the end of the century at the level of 650 persons per square kilometre, which will be five times the average density in China at present and not very far from the density in South Korea (493). The pressure exerted by the population actually depends on its distribution on the country's territory and the nature of economic activities, some of which may require a considerable amount of land. The effective density in China is thus more than 500 persons per square kilometre in the coastal provinces and almost 1000 in Guangdong province.

Although India's population is not as concentrated in some areas as that of its Chinese neighbour, mainly because of its history and its federal political structure, the ratio of population pressure is 9:1 between Bengal (904) and Jammu & Kashmir (99). With the exception of Kerala (819) and Tamil Nadu (478), which are in the final stage of demographic transition, there is a higher population density in the poorer states whose future gives much cause for concern, especially Bihar (880) and Uttar Pradesh (689) whose population is likely to double. The solution to this problem of population pressure therefore depends on migration to other states and urbanisation which are linked together. A city like Delhi, together with the national capital region (NCR), receives an influx of about 400,000 migrants per year, almost the same as greater Bombay in Maharashtra, while Uttar Pradesh and Bihar have a net negative migratory balance of several millions. This movement from the North and East towards the West creates a strong population pressure on some megacities because of the failure to develop medium-sized towns in a predominantly rural area. Thus, in spite of a rather low definition threshold (5,000 persons), the proportion of the urban population has increased quite slowly: by 23.3 per cent in 1981 and 27.8 per cent in 2001. But in absolute terms, the increase is quite substantial: 60 million in 1951 and 300 million today, and this increase has occurred mainly in the mega-cities. Besides, the real shift towards urbanisation is taking place now and the urban population is expected to reach the figure of 520 million by 2026 according to the most reliable estimates [Dyson et al., 2004].

The slow progress of industrialisation and associated job-creation led in the first instance to the diversification of rural jobs with about one quarter of them outside the realm of agriculture and half of them in small fairly well developed states like Punjab and Kerala. Urban growth essentially benefited the Class I cities having a population of more than one million, whose number rose from 23 in 1991 to 35 in 2001 with almost 110 million inhabitants, and then Class II cities with a population of more than 100,000. Their combined ratio rose from 57.2 per cent of the urban population in 1971 to almost 70 per cent at present to the detriment of intermediate towns having a population below 20,000. The transformation of "megacities" into a refuge for job-seeking migrants has led to their saturation with practically half their population living in slums [Dewan-Verma, 2002]. A metropolis like Delhi, having a population of barely 400,000 at the time of independence, had 8.4 million inhabitants in 1991 whose number rose to 12.8 million in 2001 and is expected to rise further to 36.2 million in 2026 making it one of the biggest cities in India, followed by greater Bombay (31.7 million as compared to 16.4 million in 2001) and Calcutta (21.3 million as compared to 13.3 million in 2001). In 2026, India will have a total of nine cities with a population of more than 10 million as compared to only three in 2001 and four cities having a population of one million in 1951. In spite of the attempts to control the growth of its megacities, especially by building new townships and industrial parks on their periphery, the present crisis in Bangalore, India's IT capital, reveals the high speed of socio-demographic transition which will stabilize only when industrialisation spreads to medium-sized towns in accordance with the recent plan envisaging the creation of 460 industrial clusters. If this does not happen, international emigration, which is at present fairly limited and selective (Gulf countries: 3.4 million and Anglo-Saxon countries: 4 million), is likely to serve as a safety valve as already seen in the case of Bangladesh, Nepal and Pakistan. This is now an important point in the ongoing debate on international outsourcing of services which provides direct and indirect employment to more than 2 million persons and their number could rise to 11 million by 2007. And finally, it is a crucial element for maintaining a sustainable environment in India considering that the present level of investment in urban amenities is barely 20 to 40 per cent of the amount required to simply maintain the relative level of the per capita infrastructure.

Table 3.2. Estimated Population of Indian States according to the Level of Demographic Transition

	In Millions			*% of Total Indian Population*		
States	**1991**	**2051**	**2101**	**1991**	**2051**	**2101**
Demographic transition almost complete						
Kerala	29,1	36	25,2	3,5%	2,2%	1,4%
Tamil Nadu	55,9	72	57	6,6%	4,4%	3,1%
Andhra Pradesh	66,5	119,9	130,5	7,9%	7,4%	7,2%
Himachal Pradesh	5,2	9,5	10,3	0,6%	0,6%	0,6%
Karnataka	45	78	85	5,3%	4,8%	4,7%
Mahrashtra	78,9	147,4	159,6	9,4%	9,1%	8,8%
Sub-total	*280,6*	*462,8*	*467,6*	33,3%	28,6%	25,8%
Demographic transition in the last stage						
Punjab	20.3	35.7	37.9	2.4%	2.2%	2.1%
West Bengal	68.1	121.9	132.0	8.1%	7.5%	7.3%
Gujarat	41.3	73.0	80.2	4.9%	4.5%	4.4%
Orissa	31.7	53.9	59.5	3.8%	3.3%	3.3%
Assam	22.4	42.0	47.0	2.7%	2.6%	2.6%
Sub-total	*183.8*	*326.5*	*356.6*	21.8%	20.2%	19.7%

Demographic transition still incomplete						
Haryana	16.5	41.1	48.8	2.0%	2.5%	2.7%
Madhya Pradesh	66.2	148.0	175.3	7.9%	9.1%	9.7%
Bihar	86.4	188.0	216.7	10.2%	11.6%	12.0%
Rajasthan	44.0	106.1	125.9	5.2%	6.6%	6.9%
Uttar Pradesh	139.1	337.0	405.0	16.5%	20.8%	22.3%
Sub-total	*352.2*	*820.2*	*971.7*	41.8%	50.6%	53.6%
All India Total	**843.3**	**1619.5**	**1812.2**	**100.0%**	**100.0%**	**100.0 %**

Source : L. & P. Visaria, EPW November 8, 2003

Changes in the Structure of Employment and GDP

So far, India has managed the overall population pressure by controlling the rate of labour participation, especially of women and so-called marginal categories (for whom a job is a secondary occupation). According to the 2001 census, the rate of participation was thus only 39.2 per cent of which 43 per cent was in rural areas and 32.2 per cent in urban areas. This genderbased discrimination is essential since there are 52.4 per cent active males in rural areas and 50.9 per cent in urban areas as compared to only 30.1 per cent and 11.6 per cent active women. Finally, out of 402.5 million active workers in 2001, 22.2 per cent were secondary workers of whom 42.8 per cent were women. But the ratio fell to 9 per cent in urban areas – 6.6 per cent for men and 21.2 per cent for women. This distortion in the cities caused by the rise in the population of younger age groups and a decrease in the fertility rate will pose a major challenge on the employment front during the coming years. The rate of participation should in fact increase from 40.4 per cent to 45.3 per cent between 2000 and 2026 [Dyson et al., 2004] mainly due to the arrival of young urban women in the permanent employment market, and accumulate due to the growth of younger age groups to raise the net availability of jobs from 407 to 643 million between the two dates, or an increase of almost 10 million per annum. However, changes in the GDP structure no longer allow the rural areas to absorb the growing work force. As a matter of fact, the number of jobs in the agricultural sector is falling by 1 to 2 per cent per annum. The primary sector in India is shrinking more slowly than in many other countries, thus maintaining the availability of jobs in rural areas. Their relative share remained stable at about 72 per cent of the active population between 1901 and 1971, and continued to be about 68 per cent between 1981 and 1991. But since then, it has decreased at a faster pace dropping to 56.7 per cent in 2000 and 51 per cent according to the provisional data for 2004, which is paradoxically quite close to China's for a per capita GDP that is less than half. It is equally true that rural areas are no longer considered a refuge as a survey conducted in 2005 shows that 40 per cent of Indian peasants would like to leave their land. The change that occurred in the primary sector in 1991 was also seen in the secondary sector. Having remained surprisingly stable between 1901 and 1991 at the level of about 12.5 per cent, it rose abruptly to 17.5 per cent of jobs in 2000 and almost 20 per cent in 2004, half the increase taking place in the construction sector and the other half in the manufacturing sector. However, the latter accounts for no more than 13 per cent of the total jobs as compared to almost 18 per cent in China. On the other hand, just as in China, the dynamism of employment in the services is an essential variable of transition. Its relative share increased by 10 points between 1981 and 2001 to reach 27 per cent of the active population in 2001 as compared to 28 per cent in China. On the development front (per capita GDP), these two countries have a fairly distinctive employment structure weighing relatively more in favour of industries and agriculture in China and more in favour of services in India.

Table 3.3. Sectorwise GDP and Employment Distribution: 1950-2005 (per cent)

		GDP			*Employment*		
		Primary	*Secondary*	*Tertiary*	*Primary*	*Secondary*	*Tertiary*
1950	100	58	15	28	72	11	17
1960	100	53	18	29	72	12	16
1970	100	46	22	32	72	11	17
1980	100	40	24	37	69	14	18
1990	100	32	27	41	67	13	21
2000	100	24	27	49	57	18	26
2005e	100	24	27	49	52	19	28

Sources: CSO and Economic Survey 2005-06.

e=estimates.

Another major difference with China is the sectoral distortion of the GDP structure. The share of the primary sector fell from 59 to 24 per cent between 1951 and 2003 with a notable increase since 1991, while the share of the secondary sector doubled to 25 per cent at the end of the period, but at a level that was twice as low as in China where the distortion occurred during the Maoist regime. The share of the services sector on the other hand registered a relative increase by moving from 28 to 35 per cent of India's GDP between 1951 and 1989 while it remained stagnant in China at 24 per cent making up for lost time only after the 1990s. In India it crossed the level of 50 per cent of the GDP in 2001 as compared to only 34 per cent in China. The comparison between the two Asian giants thus shows that while the relative productivity of services is much higher in India, it is also higher in the agricultural sector [Etienne, 1998], but the situation is just the opposite in the industrial sector, particularly in manufacturing. This situation confirms the international image of the two competing countries portraying China as the "world's workshop" and India as the "world's back-office". Finally, China's agricultural sector seems to have suffered more than India's after it was opened up to comply with WTO rules in 2001. For all that, its future is far from secure.

3.2. Indian Agriculture

An Agricultural Giant

Though it is known more for its famines, even though the last one in Bengal goes back to 1943, India is an agricultural giant. It ranks fourth in the world after China, the former Soviet Union and the United States; its total area is the seventh largest in the world but its cultivated area is second only to the United States and its rural population is second to China's: one out of five farmers in the world lives in India. It is also the world's largest producer of milk, tea and spices and the second largest producer of fruits and sugar cane (after Brazil) and the third largest producer of cereals (rice, wheat, maize, millets and sorghum) after China and the United States. Finally, it has the highest number of cattle in the world numbering almost 450 million heads, and the largest area of irrigated land. India is also gradually removing restrictions on the trade of agricultural products and even has a surplus trade balance being the world's largest exporter of tea and spices, the second largest exporter of rice and the seventh largest exporter of wheat. But it is more on the internal level that India is an agricultural giant. Thanks to its climatic and geographic diversity, 60 per cent of its total area is under cultivation: 190 million hectares as compared to 130 million in China. More than half the active population is engaged in agriculture and approximately 70 per cent of its population is rural, so that even though its agricultural GDP represented only a quarter of its total GDP in 2003, it influences at least a third of the GDP and almost half the demand as is evident in the years when the monsoon is poor. The monsoon cycle, which is an important climatic feature in the subcontinent with its summer (Kharif) and winter (Rabi) crops, has a profound influence on the fluctuations in the Indian economy as a whole and even its political history, because every important event in its past is directly related to a bad monsoon, for example 1965, 1971 and particularly 1991.

Success and Limitations of the Green Revolution

However, it has been observed that the per capita availability of cereals has been almost stagnant since Independence: 419 grams per day in the early 1950s, rising slowly to about 470 grams during the period 1996-2000, and approximately 450 grams during the last four years. Similarly, the unequal distribution of food has created a situation of endemic malnutrition affecting the country's 300 million poor. Finally, the level of nutritional deficiencies remains quite high: more than 60 per cent of the total population (half of it in rural areas) suffered from calorie deficiency in 2000; 50 per cent from lipid deficiency; almost 60 per cent (20 per cent in urban areas) from protein deficiency, pointing to the poor quality of food even in cities.

The agricultural policies adopted to meet the challenge of feeding a fast-growing population have been through three important phases. A long phase after Independence covering all crops which led to an annual increase of 1.6 per cent in the cultivated areas, of which 1.4 per cent were under cereals and 2.5 per cent under other crops, the largest area being under potatoes (+4.4 per cent) and cotton (+3.3 per cent). However, in spite of the Congress's pro-reform policy since 1935, its relative failure to bring in the required agricultural reforms led to the increase of marginal and unfertile lands due to the slow progress of irrigation. The agricultural crisis in 1965-66, which put the country's independence in peril, hastened the advent of the Green Revolution by making "self-reliance" the principal objective of the country's economic policy. This intensive phase was dependent on a series of measures including the introduction of high-yielding varieties of seeds, mainly wheat and rice, developed a few years earlier in Mexico and the Philippines. It also depended on irrigation, the widespread use of chemical fertilisers, the development of storage and distribution facilities and, finally, setting up essential institutional mechanisms like rural credit (NABARD), a price-support policy (CACP), storage of food-grains at the national level (FCI) and finally a public distribution system (PDS) officially meant to maintain prices at a low level and supply food-grains at subsidized prices to the low-income and poor population. The results were evident in the reversal of productivity figures which took precedence over the increase of the area under cultivation: the latter stabilised at the rate of +0.1 per cent per annum between 1965 and 2001, while the yield recorded an increase of +2.4 per cent as compared to +1.4 per cent. The biggest gainer was wheat (+3.2 per cent) followed by rice.

Table 3.4. India's Main Agricultural Products: Volume and Area under Cultivation

	World Rank	Million Tonnes			Million Hectares		
		1980-1981	*1990-1991*	*2002-2003*	*1980-1981*	*1990-1991*	*2002-2003*
Foodgrains		130	176	174	127	128	112
Cereals	3rd	119	162	163	104	103	91
Rice		53	74	73	40	43	40
Wheat		36	55	65	22	24	25
Jowar		10	12	7	16	14	9
Bajra		5	7	5	12	11	8
Maize		7	9	10	6	6	6
Others		4	5	3	8	6	3
Pulses	2nd	11	14	11	23	25	20
Gram		4	5	4	7	8	6
Tur		2	2	2	3	4	3
Others		6	7	5	13	14	11
Oilseeds		9	19	15	18	24	21
Groundnut (in shell)		5	8	4	7	8	6
Rapeseed & mustard		2	5	4	4	6	5
Others		2	6	7	7	10	11
Cotton @	4th	7	10	9	8	7	8
Jute @		7	8	10	1	1	1
Sugarcane (cane weight)	2nd	154	241	282	3	4	4
Tea	1st	1	1	1	0	0	1
Coffee	6th	0,1	0,2	0,3	0,2	0,2	0,3
Milk	1st	32	54	88			
Eggs (Billion units)		10	21	42			

@ Million bales (cotton: 170kg and jute:180 kg)
Source: Economic Survey 2004/05 (financial years)

Thanks to this change, India gained on several fronts [Dorin & Landy, 2002]. Due to the spurt in food-grain production, it was able to build up a strategic reserve of 58 million tonnes in 2002 of which almost 50 per cent was either exported (13 million tonnes) or sold in the open market (5 million tonnes), and a major portion (10 million tonnes) was set aside for distribution to the underprivileged sections of the population through "Food for Work" programmes (Rs.54 per day for work on public sites in 2005, of which Rs.14 was paid in cash with 6 kg of wheat). The total cereal production rose from 82 million tonnes in 1960 to a record 212 million tones in 2003-04.

The plantations, a legacy of the colonial rule, were developed for the cultivation of spices and condiments, tea, coffee, cotton and sugar cane. Finally, there were a few other successful revolutions such as the White Revolution in the field of milk production brought about by setting up an innovative cooperative system in Gujarat (Amul), which allowed millions of marginal milk-producers to sell their daily yield of a few litres to the milk-cooperative; the Blue Revolution in the field of fisheries, especially inland fisheries, which helped fish production to catch up with the population growth in the mid-1980s. Finally, poultry-farming grew rapidly during the same period leading to a stupendous increase in the production of eggs which are now commonly available even in small corner-shops in both cities and villages.

On the other hand, the system developed in the 1960s gradually faced severe constraints as output fell and unexpected developments made it necessary to give a fresh impetus to agriculture at the beginning of the new millennium. The constraints affected the crops neglected by the Green Revolution, especially pulses which are an essential part of the diet in a country where more than one third of the population is strictly vegetarian and three quarters mostly vegetarian. The production of pulses has stagnated at the level of 13 to15 million tonnes since 1960. Similarly, the failure of the Yellow Revolution in the domain of oilseeds in the mid-1980s resulted in increased imports to satisfy the demand for vegetable oil which has soared, as in other developing countries, with rapidly growing incomes. Finally, the production of fruits increased considerably, but it is estimated that only 20 per cent of the produce is properly marketed due to losses caused by an archaic distribution and processing network.

As for the Green Revolution itself, the normal fall in output was made worse by a decline in public investment in agriculture since the mid-1980s, and particularly investment on irrigation even as the water problem became more severe due to growing population pressure and the unexpected effects of chemical pollution that are a cause of great concern. While the potential yield of hybrid varieties of rice is 40 to 58 quintals per hectare, in India it was only 29.3 quintals as compared to 63.2 in China and 88.8 in Egypt (a world record). The negative effects of the existing system created a vicious circle with subsidies for cereal cultivation leading to an immense increase in their production cost: Rs. 28.5 billion in 1991-92 and almost Rs.140 billion in 2003, that is more than 6 per cent of the GDP. The model also failed because the average size of cultivated plots became smaller over the years and the number of people dependent on each plot increased. The average size of a cultivated plot came down from 2.88 hectares in 1953 to 1.41 in 1995 and is rapidly approaching a low of one hectare. The Indian government is fully aware of the outcome of these portents and is making preparations, though rather hesitantly at present, to launch a new agricultural revolution which would involve the adoption of new technologies, particularly genetically modified crops, and integration with the international market which is advantageous for high value-added products. This shift in the Indian position was noticeable during the recent international trade negotiations where it tried to find a compromise between the asymmetrical globalisation policy of the rich countries and its own policy of self-reliance dependent on the self-sufficiency of rural masses having no other employment opportunities at present.

3.3. Industry

While China occupies a central position in the world manufacturing industry, India has been much slower in taking off in this field. However, recent signs of acceleration following the liberalisation of the economy in 1991 reveal a pattern of industrialisation that is totally different from the Chinese model of export-oriented mass production. The Indian model is less specialised, less liberalised, but more inclined to variety and a high added value per unit, as far as its modern sector is concerned, in order to make up for structural handicaps such as the lack of adequate infrastructure. But it still lags far behind in the unorganized sector.

Structure of Indian Industry: Family Groups and the Unorganized Sector

The ideological choices made at the time of Independence are still evident in India's industrial structure. The public sector, which did not exist at the time of Independence, made such rapid progress that it represented one third of the added value during the 1990s, before liberalisation. It still represents a little more than 25 per cent in highly concentrated units: 5 per cent of the country's enterprises but almost one third of the total capital. Political reservations about privatisation that persist even today have led to a phase of gradual consolidation around a hard core of basic industries like oil (IOC, ONGC), steel (SAIL), petrochemicals (BP) and telecommunications (BSNL), but which are now exposed to competition from the private sector. Disinvestment in other sectors was slow, especially in the states where half the public sector enterprises are concentrated, but which now find themselves incapable of subsidising them.

At the other extreme, investments by large private sector industries were under strict government control until the first phase of relaxation in the 1980s under Indira Gandhi. They were the principal gainers when reforms were introduced in 1991, even though the intensification of domestic and foreign competition led to two upheavals. Firstly, a large part of the traditional family-run groups incapable of adapting themselves to the new situation either disappeared or made way for a new generation of more aggressive private family-run groups (Bharti, Pantaloon, etc.) or foreign groups taking advantage of the liberalisation of sectors like the automobile sector (Suzuki and Hyundai), telecommunications (Hutch), cement (Lafarge), or those who took advantage of the recent relaxation of laws to set up joint-ventures with foreign companies (Hero-Honda, Toyota-Kirloskar, Michelin-Apollo etc.). Competition further obliged the large Indian groups to focus on their strong points and gradually give up the conglomerate structure fostered by the industrial licensing policy. The result was paradoxical with an unprecedented expansion of some sectors, which did not however create too many new jobs, and even their gradual disappearance from the list of major companies quoted on the stock market. India's peculiarity continues to be the predominance of family-owned groups among its major enterprises, even though greater professionalism is now evident in their management as seen in the House of Tatas, the country's largest private group where 68 year old Ratan Tata is now the only Tata on the Company's Board of Directors. As compared to China, this is one of India's plus points as it has set itself the objective of putting at least two or three Indian companies among the world's top fifty in every sector in the coming years.

Another sign of the continuation of past preferences is the importance given to small industries. They account for almost 40 per cent of the country's industrial production, about one third of which is exported, and constitute the biggest jobproviders (65 per cent) with an annual growth of 4 to 5 per cent which makes them an essential safety valve, especially in rural areas where three fourths of small and medium industries are concentrated. The latter are nevertheless faced with the difficulty of adapting themselves to the changing situation following the acceleration of reforms. Historically speaking, the "Small-Scale Industry" was protected right from the time the first Industrial Policy Resolution was framed in 1948 in the name of the Gandhian ideal of village industries, but also to economize on capital which was to be invested in the public sector. Defined either according to the maximum number of employees (10) or the ceiling on capital, gradually entire sectors came under the SSI: 837 when it was at its peak in 1983 covering about 7,500 products including a wide variety of textiles, automobile parts and food and health products. The SSI is in fact two-dimensional with a traditional component based on crafts using very little or no machinery and a modern component representing almost 75 per cent of the production but only one third of the jobs provided. Its rapid development due to the reservation of certain products and labour regulations (that sometimes justify all kinds of excesses) has led to the emergence of specialised townships as in Ludhiana in Punjab, where 63 per cent of India's total production of bicycle components and 92 per cent of knitted woollen goods are manufactured. There are hundreds of similar clusters of modern SMEs, many of which are actually working under contract for big industries with the aim of bypassing the rigid labour laws governing the organized sector. The liberalisation of the Indian economy has made the country aware of the negative effects of the reservation system which leads to a fall in quality below the optimum level, poor working conditions and the absence of economies of scale. Towards this end, a gradual de-reservation policy was introduced in 1997, the most important measure being the Textile Policy of 2000 for the garment industry, so that the number of reserved sectors came down to 605 in October 2004. But due to stiff social and political resistance, the Indian industrial scenario will take a long time to change.

Sectoral Post-liberalisation Dynamics

The sectoral legacy of the pre-liberalisation industrial policy is on the whole a fairly well-balanced structure, one third of which consists of basic sectors (petrochemicals, steel and cement), one third of intermediate products (chemicals, partially processed metals and wood products) and one third of durable and especially non-durable consumer goods (6 per cent as compared to 24 per cent). On the other hand, the capital goods sector accounting for 9 per cent of the total production has not fulfilled its promise as in other developing countries which have followed the same kind of import-substitution strategy. The liberalisation in 1991 nevertheless influenced the country's industrial dynamics due to growing specialisation within each sector; the need to be competitive both within the country and at the international level has reshaped industrial thinking according to the sector's ability to adapt itself to the diversion of labour in the international sphere. Unlike China, which has clearly decided to opt for labour-intensive industries due to the availability of cheap labour and then move up the manufacturing chain keeping in mind the labour situation in Asia [Boillot & Michelon, 2001], Indian industry is trying to integrate itself more adroitly with world competition by developing its outsourcing capabilities in technological niche areas, especially because it still does not have a sufficiently large domestic market capable of paying for these services.

As for basic industries, petrochemicals and steel are fine examples of an established competitive advantage which permits Indian industry to serve the domestic market in addition to exporting its surplus production to other countries including China. Although India is increasingly dependent on oil imports, one of the world's biggest refineries is located in Gujarat thanks to the huge investments made by the Reliance Group in the 1980s. Further, public sector groups IOC and ONGC are slowly emerging as future world leaders in the realm of oil and gas due to an aggressive long-term policy which enables them to acquire exploration rights in areas as far-off as Africa (Sudan), Central Asia (Kazakhstan) and Russia. Finally, India has become more or less independent in various processing activities. Indian groups manufacturing synthetic yarn and paints (Asian Paints) are among the world's leading companies exporting their products even to China. The polyester group Jindal, which ranks fifth in the world after the Korean company SKC, is expected to double its production capacity during the coming years. It already exports 70 per cent of its polyester film used as packing material, of which half is sold to Europe.

In the steel sector, India has a long way to go before it can figure among the world's largest producers having a capacity of only 37 million tones in 2004 as compared to China's 250 million tonnes. But it produces enough for its own needs (31 million tonnes) and has to import barely 1.5 million tonnes, while its exports have increased rapidly during the last few years (5 million tonnes in 2003-04 half of which was exported to China), and TISCO (part of the Tata Group) is supposed to be the world's most efficient steel-producer today. Thanks to abundant reserves of high quality iron ore in Orissa, the Korean group Posco is keen

Table 3.5. The First 50 Business Groups by the Market Cap and Type of Control

rang	*Name*	*Market Cap 2004/05 Bn USD*	*Business House /Public Sector/ Foreign*	*Original Place*	*Community*
1.	RELIANCE INDUSTRIES	28,2	Reliance	Gujarat	Vaishnava gujarati
2.	ONGC (OIL & NATURAL GAS CORP)	23,0	public sector		
3.	TATA	19,9	Tata	Gujarat (Iran)	Parsi
4.	BHARTI TELE-VENTURES	13,8	Bharti Telecom	Punjab	Baniya punjabi
5.	IOC (INDIAN OIL CORP).	10,8	public sector		
6.	INFOSYS TECHNOLOGIES	8,5	Infosys	Tamil Nadu	Brahmin Iyer/Iyengar
7.	WIPRO	8,3	Wipro technologies	Gujarat	Bora (musulman)
8.	AV Birla	6,9	AV Birla	Rajasthan	Baniya marwari
9.	HINDUSTAN LEVER	6,3	foreign		
10.	SBI (STATE BANK OF INDIA)	5,8	public sector		
11.	HDFC (banque)	5,6	HDFC		
12.	ITC	5,5	I.T.C.		
13.	RANBAXY LABORATORIES	4,8	Ranbaxy	Punjab	Shatriya sikh

No.	Company	Value	Group	State	Community
14.	ICICI BANK	4,4	ICICI		
15.	HCL TECHNOLOGIES	4,4	HCL	Tamil Nadu	Nadar
16.		4,3	Bajaj	Rajasthan	Baniya marwari
17.	STERLITE INDUSTRIES (INDIA)	4,2		Rajasthan	Baniya marwari
18.	GAIL (INDIA)	3,6	public sector		
19.	STEEL AUTHORITY OF INDIA	3,2	public sector		
20.	BHEL (BHARAT HEAVY ELECTRICALS)	3,0	public sector		
21.	SUZUKI MARUTI UDYOG	2,8	foreign		
22.	HPCL (HINDUSTAN PETROLEUM CORP).	2,7	public sector		
23.	BPCL (BHARAT PETROLEUM CORP.)	2,5	public sector		
24.	LARSEN & TOUBRO	2,5	Larsen & Toubro Group	Maharastra	Brahmin marathi
25.	SATYAM COMPUTER SERVICES	2,3	Satyam	Tamil Nadu	Brahmin Iyer/Iyengar
26.	NATIONAL ALUMINIUM CO	2,2	public sector		
27.	HERO HONDA MOTORS	2,1	Hero Group	Punjab	Baniya punjabi
28.	NEYVELI LIGNITE CORP.	1,9			
29.	United Breweries (UB)	1,8	United Breweries Group	Karnataka	Brahmin - Chetia Naga
30.	CIPLA	1,6		Gujarat	Bora (musulman)
31.	SUN PHARMACEUTICAL INDS.	1,5		Rajasthan	Baniya marwari
32.	LM THAPAR	1,5	LM Thapar	Punjab	Shatriya punjabi

33.	ABB	1,5	Asea Brown Boveri Inc		
34.	NICHOLAS PIRAMAL INDIA	1,5	Nicholas Piramal	Rajasthan	Baniya marwari
35.	DR. REDDY'S LABORATORIES	1,4		Andhra Pradesh	Brahmins
36.	ASIAN PAINTS (INDIA	1,4	Asain paints (India)	Gujarat	Choksi gujarati
37.	WOCKHARDT	1,4	Wockhardt Group	Gujarat	Bora (musulman)
38.	Murugappa	1,3	Murugappa	Tamil Nadu	Brahmin Chetia Naga
39.	ZEE TELEFILMS	1,3	Rajasthan	Baniya	marwari
40.	ESSAR	1,2	ESSAR	Rajasthan	Ruia marwari
41.	NESTLE INDIA	1,2	foreign		
42.	GUJARAT AMBUJA CEMENTS	1,2		Rajasthan	Baniya marwari
43.	BIOCON	1,2	Biocon India Group	Gujarat	Gujarati
44.	jaiPrakash	1,2		Maharastra	Baniya mahrati
45.	Jindal	1,1		Rajasthan	Marwari
46.	BK BIRLA	1,1	BK Birla	Rajasthan	Baniya marwari
47.	Wadia	1,1	Wadia Group	Gujarat (Iran)	Parsi
48.	Godrej Consumers products	1,0	Godrej	Gujarat (Iran)	Parsi
49.	VSNL (VIDESH SANCHAR NIGAM)	1,0	Tata	Gujarat (Iran)	Parsi
50.	RP GONEKA	1,0	Goneka	Rajasthan	Jain marwari

Sources: Collection of Business India and CSH, Le patronat en Inde [2000]

on investing US$ 12.4 billion to set up an integrated 12 million tonne steel plant, and with higher bids from the Tata Group and Mittal (LNM), it is expected that by 2010 this state alone will have an installed capacity of 53 million tones, equal to the domestic demand in 2011. In all, India is expected to produce 100 million tonnes of steel by 2020 even though experts believe that its potential capacity could go up to 200 million tonnes.

As regards other metals, it is now the world's second highest producer of chromium and the fifth highest producer of iron and bauxite.

In the two- and four-wheeler sector, India made a break-through in the 1980s with the relaxation of the regime compelling it to manufacture on a small scale models that were designed in the 1950s (Enfield and Austin/Ambassador). Taking advantage of a flourishing domestic market, the Indian two-wheeler industry increased its production from 447,000 units per annum in 1980 to almost 6 million units in 2004 becoming the world's second largest producer thanks to the efforts of Indian companies like Bajaj and Hero-Honda which had built up a network of international alliances with Japanese producers. As for trucks, the two big Indian producers, Telco (Tata Group) and Ashok Leyland (the original British company was bought out by the Hinduja family), produce between them almost 300,000 units per annum and Telco has recently become an international company by acquiring the truck division of Samsung as well as a Spanish company. In the automobile sector, production crossed the level of one million units in 2004 as compared to 220,000 in 1990 and barely 50,000 in 1980. Foreign producers now dominate the market, particularly the Japanese automaker Suzuki which launched its first joint-venture in 1984 (controlling 55 per cent of the market), followed by the Korean Hyundai (100 per cent independent) only in 2001. Then came Toyota with an alliance with the Kirloskar Group, while Renault is expected to bring out its global model Lagan in 2006 in alliance with the Mahindra Group. But the local groups are reorganising themselves. Apart from the alliances mentioned above, Telco (now Tata Motors), the first Indian company to cross the level of 100,000 units in 2004 as a sub-contractor for Rover, joined hands with Fiat in early 2005, and expects to launch the first totally Indian car costing less than Rs.100,000 (€ 2,000) by 2008. India, which specialises in the production of small cars, has become an export base from 2003 (US$ 2 billion in 2004), and expects to become an international hub in this segment, especially because its R&D costs are ten times lower (the development costs of the Tata Indica were only US$ 140 million) and it already has a fast-growing auto components industry having adopted the outsourcing strategy following in the footsteps of the IT sector.

The same strategy of serving niche areas and outsourcing are followed by the pharmaceuticals and biotechnology sectors where India is emerging as a world leader having specialized in generic drugs and outsourcing for leading world manufacturers. It has the largest number of production sites approved by USFDA: 63 as compared to 25 in China and Spain. CIPLA, for example, produces the cheapest anti-HIV drugs in the world and exports 40 per cent of its products to 140 countries. The turnover of Ranbaxy Laboratories, India's largest pharmaceutical company, has crossed the figure of US$ 1 billion and in 2004 it acquired the French company RPG Aventis for US$ 50 million. In the biotechnology sector, the industry employs only 9,000 persons with an annual turnover of almost US$ 1 billion. But the five major players in this sector, including Bio-pharma and Biocon, are likely to increase their turnover five times by 2010 making India one of the world's biggest hubs in this domain with an R&D cost that is five times lower than in developed countries. This explains why an investment of US$ 1 to 10 billion and a creation of a million jobs is expected in this sector by 2010 thanks partly to the efforts of multinationals as well as Indian companies taking advantage of their geographical proximity to Bangalore, the Mecca of biotechnology in India.

Table 3.6. Distribution of Factories according to Size of Labor Forceand Capital

	No. of Factories	*Employment*		*Productive Capital*	*Net Value added*
Value of Plant and Machinery 1/		Workers	Employees 2/	Rs. Crores	Rs. Crores
Tiny Factories (Up to Rs.5 lakhs)	59,131	1,396	1,598	8,297	6,281
Small Factories (Rs. 5lakhs to 100 lakhs)	56,496	1,920	1,453	39,748	18,890
Medium Factories (Rs.100 lakhs to 1000 lakhs)	13,913	1,676	2,242	80,239	31,534
Large Factories (Rs. 1000lakhs to 10000 lakhs)	5,369	1,925	2,672	207,208	49,934
Very large Factories (Rs. 10000 lakhs & above)	642	688	961	251,038	49,308
Total	135,551	7,605	9,926	586,530	155,947

Source: Compiled and computed from Annual Survey of Industries (1997-98)

Note: 1. Productive capital is total fixed capital and working capital

2. Employees include workers, supervisors, managerial cadre, etc

1 Lakh = 100,000 and 1 Crore = 10 million.

It should be noted that among the modern sectors in the process of globalisation, India is lagging far behind other countries in the electronic sector in spite of the collective desire for progress that has been evident for a long time. While the production of household appliances has grown by leaps and bounds following the entry of big Korean (Samsung and LG) and Swedish (Whirlpool) multinationals attracted by the hundreds of millions of consumers, and has also stimulated Indian producers like Videocon now facing pressure from Chinese companies in this segment, this has not happened so far in the electronics sector. The fact that India's total turnover was less than US$ 10 billion in 2004, or five times lower than Chinese exports in this sector, points to India's weakness in the mass production of standardised goods as compared to its Chinese competitor forming an integral part of the Asian circuit starting from Japan and passing through Korea and Singapore.

Pressure from China is also felt in the garment industry which is still India's leading industrial sector accounting for almost 11 per cent of the production in the manufacturing sector, or 4 per cent of its GDP and one third of its exports, in addition to providing employment to 35 million persons. It is thus the country's largest foreign-exchange earner together with IT. Further, experts believe that the abolition of textile quotas in January 2005 will greatly benefit India. According to Mckinsey, it could become the world's second largest supplier of textile goods after China, with its exports rising to US$ 25-30 billion by 2013; but this will be possible only if the restructuring of the sector continues and the country improves its infrastructure. However, this will not suffice to maintain employment at the current level and represents one of the major challenges faced by Indian industry whose irreversible choice of globalisation has not yet brought any benefits in the form of increased employment even as hordes of unqualified youngsters enter the job market at the rate of 6-8 million per year [Planning Commission, 2002a]. This will continue until a similar change takes place in the consumer goods industries, which are still very traditional and not yet internationalised. But things will be speeded up by the ongoing revolution in the retail sector after its recent liberalisation, the proliferation of shopping malls and the emergence of a few big Indian retail chains like Pantaloon bound to be followed by international chains like Wal-Mart, Metro and Carrefour.

3.4. Revolution in the Services Sector

A distinctive feature of India's growth since the 1990s is the significant contribution of services going much beyond the traditional transition models of the type proposed by Kuznets or Chenery. From 1951 to 1980, India's services sector grew on an average by 4.5 per cent per annum as compared to an industrial growth of 5.3 per cent. The 1980s decade, however, witnessed a growth of 6.6 per cent per annum, but it was still slightly lower than the rate of industrial growth. It increased subsequently to 7.5 per cent per annum during the 1990s, stabilising at 8-9 per cent per annum and contributing more than 60 per cent to the change in India's GDP. An assessment of India's GDP and its active population in the tertiary sector reveals that the Indian model is rather distorted [Gordon and Gupta, 2004] as compared to the standard model. At the development level, it represented 51.5 per cent of the GDP in 2003 as compared to approximately 40 per cent in countries having almost the same per capita income, but less than 25 per cent of jobs, with even a relative decrease during the 1990s. As a result, the relative productivity of the sector is one of the highest in the world when you compare the increase in its contribution to the country's growth to its contribution to job-creation.

Table 3.7. Output and Employment in the Services Sector during the 1990s

	growth per cent	per cent GDP 2000
Business services	19.8	1.1
Communication	13.6	2.0
Banks	12.7	6.3
Hotels and Restaurants	9.3	1.0
Health & Education	8.4	5.5
Wholesale and Retail Trade	7.3	13.7
Others	7.1	0.7
Transport	6.9	4.3
Insurance	6.7	0.7
Public Administration, Defence	6.0	6.1
Legal Services	5.8	0.0
Housing, Real Estate	5.0	4.5
Community, Social and Personal Services	5.0	1.1
Railways	3.6	1.1
Total	**7.5**	**48.0**

Source : Gordon and Gupta (2003).

Data regarding the productivity of sub-sectors confirm the singular position of services in India's economy due to the sector's relatively decreasing share in the use of the country's capital and a fall in its relative prices, especially in the communications, banking, insurance and hospitality sectors. This is exactly the role played by the manufacturing industry in the Chinese model whose relative productivity is twice the average productivity of the country. These figures reinforce the idea of a future division of the world between China as "the world's workshop" and India as "the world centre of emerging services" even though this 21st century economic Yalta is still in its formative stage. Although the services revolution in India is associated with Information Technology Enabled Services (ITES) and Business Process Outsourcing (BPO), in 2003 these services constituted less than 2 per cent of India's GDP and hence less than 4 per cent of the services sector with only 650,000 direct employees. The post-1990 dynamic had a profound effect on all modern services enabling India to become the world's outsourcing hub even in sectors like health, financial and legal services and tourism. Those who are known as "fast movers" thus saw their share in the whole commercial tertiary sector increase from 25 per cent in the 1980s to one third in 2000 and it will account for half by 2010. Services provided to enterprises are also growing at an annual rate of more than 20 per cent since the 1990s, closely followed by communication services (15 per cent) and finally the financial sector (13 per cent) of which more than 20 per cent are non-banking services. It is believed that the internal and external liberalisation in the 1980s and 1990s is responsible for this premature revolution in India's services sector on two different levels. On the international level, the growing externalisation by enterprises of their service related activities, together with a communications revolution, permitted the rapid development of offshore outsourcing in a country having a rich reserve of human resources like India whose institutes and universities produce 2.5 million graduates every year. On the domestic front, the failure to create industrial jobs led to an excess of qualified man-power and a high pressure on salaries as a whole. Thus in 2005, a young graduate employed in a BPO company earned a starting salary of €150-200 per month while a software engineer earned a little more than twice this amount (about € 900 for a project manager). For all that, can India afford to neglect the industrial sector and hope to leap directly into the post-industrial economy? Will its education system and its human resources allow it to maintain the same pace of growth as during the last few years? Many questions remain to be answered as we shall see in the following chapters.

4

Growth and Development

India often reminds you of a schizophrenic. On the one hand, you have a modern India that provides software professionals to the entire world and whose rich hold the most lavish wedding receptions for their daughters. On the other hand, there are hundreds of millions of poor. Optimists talk of the emergence of an affluent middle class – as evidenced by the growing size of hoardings – in support of the theory that growth has speeded up thanks to the trickledown effect of the reforms launched in the 1990s. Others, generally belonging to Indian ruling circles, claim that India is trailing behind China because of the difference in the methods used by democratic and totalitarian regimes to tackle the problem of mass poverty. In fact, according to the Indian Nobel laureate, economist Amartya Sen, this theory does not do much credit to India, even though his wider concept of development as freedom makes him sceptical about the superiority of China's progress [Drèze & Sen, 2002]. So is India doomed to mass poverty? Does the acceleration of growth depend on mechanisms affecting all the different strata of its population? What are the obstacles in the way of increasing its growth rate?

4.1. Poverty in India

One Third of the Population is Poor

How many poor people are there in India? Nobody knows or, to be more precise, it depends on how you define poverty. Like all other countries, India has its own definition of the poverty line (PL) defined by the minimum number of calories needed to maintain the subsistence level: 2,400 calories per day per adult in rural areas and

2,100 calories in urban areas to which is added a small allowance for non-food items. Converted into dollars at the prevalent exchange rate this amounted to an income of respectively US$ 0.18 and 0.21 in 2003, but it actually came to US$ 0.97 and 1.13 when calculated in terms of domestic prices parity of purchasing power or (PPP). According to this definition, the last official estimate goes back to the 55th round (1999-2000) of the National Sample Survey which reported that 26 per cent of India's population, or 260 millions, lived well below the poverty line. The change in the methods followed by the NSS has however led many experts to place the figure for that very year at 28.6 per cent [Datt & Ravaillon, 2002], while others question the relevance of this calorie level which is low and does not take into account real nutritional requirements. Finally, the absolute poverty line has other limitations. On the one hand, even the situation below the PL is inequitable. According to the 2004 FAO Report, the number of undernourished people was 221 million in India in 2000-2002 as compared to 142 million in China and a total of 814 million in the whole world. On the other hand, the inequitable distribution of income and consumption gave rise to the idea of a relative poverty line representing, for example, the proportion of the population living below the mean income level.

For purposes of international comparison, the most commonly used standards are the proportion of population living on at least one dollar per day (in terms of PPP) to signify abject poverty and two dollars a day according to the poverty line adopted by the United Nations (UNDP). According to its latest report (2004), 34.7 per cent of India's population lived below the first poverty line and 79.9 per cent below the second, or approximately 365 and 840 million persons in absolute figures. The development that has taken place since independence is nonetheless quite significant. Almost 55 per cent of the Indian population lived below the PL between 1951 and 1955 and more than 50 per cent between 1970 and 1974, but there was a rapid fall during 1980-1990 decade. The present pace of decline is about 1 per cent per annum, but in a situation where the GDP is going up by 6 per cent, the proportion of the population living on less than US$ 1 per day will be 28 per cent in 2015, much higher than the official target of 22 per cent fixed for the new millennium in 2000 and reiterated at the Monterrey Summit in 2002.

Similarly, India's performance in terms of reduction of poverty is not particularly creditable as compared to other countries, especially its neighbours, with the exception of Pakistan. For example, during the "lost decade" of the 1990s, the rate of reduction of extreme poverty was much faster in Bangladesh. In comparison with China in particular, the difference is now quite disturbing because, according to the calorie-based definition, the number of rural poor is supposed to have come down from 260 million in 1978 to 28 million in 2003. The proportion of the poor is thus supposed to have dropped from 7 per cent to 3 per cent of the population during the1990s enabling China to reach its millennium target 15 years before the anticipated date. However, UNDP points out that as compared to other countries, 16.6 per cent of China's population is still living below the first poverty line of US$ 1 per day and 46.7 per cent below the second line of US$ 2 per day. This means a ratio of 1:2 in comparison with India, which is close to the difference in per capita GDP or the level of relative malnutrition calculated by FAO (11 per cent of the population in China as compared to 21 per cent in India).

Table 4.1. Poverty in India and Some Other Countries in 2002

	1$/day	2$/day	NPL*
Nepal	37.7	82.5	42.0
Bangladesh	36.0	82.8	49.6
India	34.7	79.9	28.6
Senegal	26.3	67.8	64.0
China	16.6	46.7	4.6
Brazil	8.2	22.4	17.4
Sri Lanka	6.6	45.4	25.0

Source : World Bank, 2004.

NPL=National Poverty Line computed by each country.

Box - Chapter 4: Indian Economy and the Caste System

A caste is generally defined on the basis of three principles which differentiate it from the notion of a social class or a socio-professional group: endogamy or the custom of marrying within the same group, professional specialization and, finally, rigid hierarchy. The term was coined by the Portuguese in the fifteenth century to describe an Indian society organized along strict hierarchical lines based on the principles of purity (*chasta*) going back 2,000 years to the Laws of Manu. In the course of time, the notion of caste would spread far beyond India's borders and designate any social group based more or less on the three principles mentioned above (e.g. Boston Brahmins). But it gives rise to a lot of misunder-standing in the modern Indian context and is often confused with purely theoretical models like the one devised by Louis Dumont whose famous "*Homo hierarchicus*" is essentially based on an analysis of ancient texts to establish the universal principles of social organisation. This also applies to Georges Akerlof's book (published in 1984) on castes and races which simply demonstrates the purely economic reasons behind such social systems. On the prescriptive level, we may finally recall the pessimistic theory advanced by the Swedish economist Gunnar Myrdal [Asian Drama, 1968] who believed, like Mancur Olson, that castes were putting a brake on India's economic development and would do so in the future.

However, India's economy did take off even though its castes have not disappeared. On the contrary, they are adapting themselves to the current situation, especially in the political realm [Jaffrelot, 2005], and individuals generally express their identity in terms of their caste as seen in the matrimonial columns of newspapers. Nevertheless, in actual practice, castes can no longer be reduced to the four *Varnas* or colours of the Brahmanical system, namely *Brahmans* (priests), *Kshatriyas* (warriors), *Vaishyas* (merchants) and *Shudras* (farmers) to which must be added the outcastes or *Dalits* representing one fifth of the population and some 700 tribes estimated to number about 80 million persons. Thus India is more of a mosaic consisting of 4,000 to 5,000 *Jatis* or reference groups, which in turn are divided into *Gotras* or reference families descended from a common ancestor with the *Jatis* governed by the endogamic principle and the *Gotras* by the exogamic principle. These communities are distinguished by a series of interrelated variables of affiliation ranging from religion (80 per cent Hindus), to language (more than a score of official languages), region (29 states and 603 districts) and finally socio-professional origin as in the case of trading families that form the backbone of modern Indian capitalism (Tata, Birla, Bajaj, etc.).

In the countryside, and even more in towns, this social system is even today at the root of the class struggle in the administrative and political domains and involves very concrete stakes like positive discrimination (admission to educational institutions and job reservation) and gaining political power, which has turned castes into "rather flexible political agencies creating new identities" (Sunil Khilnani, *The Idea of India*). At the individual level, the caste system, as a factor determining the social and economic order, continues to be very significant in remote rural areas but tends to get dissipated as you approach urban centres due to the increasing fluidity of the modern labour market. Even though social and cultural barriers persist, competition is on the increase following the liberalisation of India's economy and its need for structural mobility (both regional and professional). Even in the business world, new groups like Bharti, Infosys and Wipro are threatening the old established communities through greater professionalism, which has also benefited members of Scheduled Castes (constituting 16 per cent of the population) and "Other Backward Castes" (OBC representing half the total population) who have taken advantage of the official discourse on democracy to compete for power with the former privileged classes.

Nevertheless, the caste system remains a paradox of modern India, not only as an instrument of the struggle to change the established order but also as a conservative strategy to defend the positions acquired with the expost-facto rationalisation of the explosion of arranged marriages accompanied by a rise in dowries.

The Economics of Caste and of the Rate Race and Other Woeful Tales, George A. Akerlof, Oxford University Press 1984; Mancur OLSON, The Logic of Collective Action: Public Goods and the Theory of Groups, Harvard University Press, 1st ed. 1965.

Mediocre Index of Human Development

Expressing growth and the quality of development as a simple poverty index may appear somewhat questionable. Since the publication of Amartya Sen's pioneering work in his magnum opus "Development as Freedom" [1999], UNDP has drawn inspiration from his wider methodology and has been including for the past few years a Human Development Index in its Annual Report on Human Development. So with an index of 0.59 in the 2004 UNDP classification, India finds itself at a mediocre level in the world scale being ranked 127th among the 175 countries that have been covered and midway between the average index for developing countries (0.66) and the lowest group, namely Sub-Saharan Africa (0.468). Even in the subcontinent, it is placed third behind Maldives and Sri Lanka. Finally, it is way behind China, with a world ranking of 104 and a HDI of 0.721, whose 1980 index was equal to what India would achieve twenty years later. Once again, it is necessary to draw attention to the marked difference between various Indian states because Kerala is on the same level as China, somewhat like all the other southern states, while the famous BIMARU states of Bihar, Madhya Pradesh, Rajasthan and Uttar Pradesh are on the same level as Sub-Saharan Africa. This marked difference in development is largely responsible for India's schizophrenic image as people tend to forget its continental dimensions.

Table 4.2. Human Development Index in India and Some Other Countries

*Rank***		*Life Expectancy*	*Education*	*GDP*
84	Maldives	0.70	0.91	0.65
94	China	0.76	0.83	0.64
96	Sri Lanka	0.79	0.83	0.60
127	India	0.64	0.59	0.55
134	Bhutan	0.63	0.48	0.50
138	Bangladesh	0.60	0.45	0.47
140	Nepal	0.58	0.50	0.44
142	Pakistan	0.60	0.40	0.49
	Developing Countries	0.66	0.71	0.62
	South Asia*	0.64	0.62	0.54
	Sub-sahara Africa	0.35	0.56	0.48

Source: United Nations, UNDP [2004] Human Development Report.
*Calculated average ;** Rank among 177 countries, highest score = 1, Norway in 2004.

If we take into account the various components, the maximum difference is seen in the field of education where the index is only 0.57 as compared to the average index of 0.70 for developing countries, 0.84 for China and 0.56 for Sub- Saharan Africa. It is evidently a severe handicap which prevents India from taking advantage of the window of opportunity opening up in the demographic sphere and maintaining the present pace of development in the outsourcing of services. The literacy rate may undoubtedly have risen from 18.3 per cent to 65.4 per cent of the total population between 1951 and 2001, but in absolute numbers India had almost 355 million illiterates at the time of the last census as compared to 324 million in 1991. Significant efforts have been made nonetheless during the last twenty years with an official rate of 93.4 per cent school-going children at the primary level. But these official statistics provided by state governments seem rather dubious to specialists. The fact is that the literacy rate has reached only 41 per cent because of the high rate of school dropouts. Out of every 100 children admitted to Class 1, only 40 reach Class V and 23 reach Class VII. In addition, the dice are heavily loaded against the girl child. The national literacy rate for women in rural areas was thus only 21 per cent in

2001 but much lower at 6.4 per cent in a poor state like Rajasthan and 11.8 per cent in Bihar. Besides, it should be kept in mind that these figures are distorted towards the higher side. In the country as a whole, the literacy rate was 76 per cent for men and 52 per cent for women.

At the same time, India's image as a land of clever people is equally real. The severe inequalities in the primary and secondary education system where private, elitist schools have an edge over government-run schools are now spreading even in the sphere of higher education. In 1982, 9 per cent of young people in the 20-24 age group, or about three times the average for developing countries, went in for higher education. And this number was only one third of the average for advanced countries. The mass effect explains the high visibility of Indian university graduates at the international level. Today, the number is close to 15 per cent with an annual turnover of 2.6 million university graduates, of which 200,000 are engineers and 300,000 have equivalent qualifications. The government which came to power in 2004 is trying to put an end to this duality by increasing the expenditure on primary education and by popularising innovative ideas like free mid-day meals for poor school-going children with even a double helping for young girls commonly used as kitchen help in poor households, especially as service enterprises are beginning to worry about the effects of an elitist education system. The Chairman of Infosys announced that during the second quarter of 2005 his company had hired 11,000 young professionals or more than five times the number of graduates produced every year by the famous Indian Institutes of Technology, which admit only 1 per cent of the candidates appearing in the Joint Entrance Exam. Considering this shortage of qualified personnel and the rapid increase of salaries in the IT sector, Narayan Murthy expressed his concern about the future because the IITs would have to produce 30,000 graduates every year to satisfy India's needs. Industrial enterprises like the giant Bharat Forge were worried at the same time about the growing shortage of engineers who are now more attracted by the IT sector. To fulfil its requirements, and with a selection rate that is nevertheless twice as low, India has to make a major effort to expand and improve its educational system. This is what China has been doing. It recently overtook India by producing more university graduates and is resolved to have 20 per cent of youngsters in the tertiary sector by 2020, or double what India will produce if circumstances remain the same.

In the health sector, the UNDP index indicates that India is close to the average index for developing countries (0.64 as compared to 0.66) and way ahead of Sub-Saharan Africa (0.36). However, life expectancy is still estimated to be only 63 to 65 years as compared to over 71 years in China and 67 years in Indonesia. Of course, it rose by more than 40 years or at the rate of 0.5 per year between 1921 and 2001. But here again, there are considerable geographical and social inequalities. It is therefore easy to understand why challenges in the public health sector figured at the top of the new government's agenda in 2004, particularly since new epidemics have taken the place of cholera and small-pox. Apart from malaria and tuberculosis, which continue to kill large numbers of people, HIV/AIDS is the major worry of the Indian rulers because it is transmitted through deeply-rooted social practices like forcing young girls into prostitution that have assumed dangerous proportions along the new quadrilateral of highways which has energized remote villages all over the subcontinent. Estimated to affect 0.8 per cent of the adult population aged between 15 and 49 years, in 2002 India had the highest incidence of HIV in Asia after Thailand and Cambodia with 4.6 million infected persons according to official figures. So India ranks second in the world, but experts estimate that the real figure is double the official figure. Keeping in mind the general lack of information and some deep-rooted traditional practices, India is threatened by a serious increase in the incidence of HIV during the coming years according to papers presented by experts at the WHO Summit in Bangkok in December 2004.

4.2. Why Doesn't Development Bring Down Poverty More Rapidly?

Although there is no doubt that the poverty level has gone down, there has been no significant change as compared to the decades preceding the1991 reforms. Using data for the period from 1958 to 1991, Ravallion and Datt [2002] have estimated that the elasticity of poverty in relation to the growth of annual consumption was already 0.9, or a level comparable to the 1990s. The slow reduction of absolute poverty in spite of the acceleration of growth is due to the conjunction of at least three factors: insufficient job-creation, geographical inequalities and social inequalities.

Growth without Jobs

In a country where 92 per cent of the active population works in the "unorganized" sector and where there are no unemployment benefits, the availability of jobs is very low. The Planning Commission however presented two reports in 2002 stressing one of the two major challenges facing India since the liberalization of its economy in 1991, one of which had a very evocative title: "Objective - ten million jobs per year" [2002]. Estimating that the unemployed population numbered 27 million in 2000 and the underemployed 35 million, its experts noted that the elasticity of employment in relation to growth had dropped to almost zero in the organized sector during the 1990s. Similarly, for the first time, the traditionally labour-intensive unorganized sector had seen a fall in its relative share of investment. All said and done, while employment increased at the rate of 2.7 per cent per annum between 1983 and 1993, job-creation fell to +1.07 per cent during the post-liberalisation period between 1993 and 2000, or from 8 million to less than 4 million in absolute value, while almost 10 million jobs were needed to satisfy the demand of the younger generation. Emigration was certainly a safety valve and according to official figures 2.4 million young people migrated between 1998 and 2004, while the total number of jobs in the organized sector dropped to 1.25 million. This was not only in the public sector (-980,000), but also in the large-scale private sector.

The first factor was the marked slow-down in the agricultural sector where employment remained stagnant at 191 million and production growth fell from 3.1 per cent during the 1980s and 1990s to barely more than 1 per cent during the following decade. This decline in the agricultural sector is at the root of the wide gap between rural and urban areas and slows down the expansion of the domestic market and the reduction of poverty. In 2002, three quarters of the poor and unemployed population lived in the rural areas with barely half of them having access to electricity and only a quarter to television as compared to two thirds of the urban population. Similarly, the number of persons owning two-wheelers was hardly 7 per cent (23.5 per cent in towns) and the number of telephone land-lines 5.3 per cent as compared to 24.3 per cent in urban areas. The second factor, which reinforces the role of rural areas as a refuge, is the low dynamism of the manufacturing sector currently engaged in an unprecedented rationalisation effort to adapt itself to the liberalization of the domestic market than in investing in new capacity to further expand the domestic market. Industrial growth slowed down perceptibly in the mid-1990s, barely crossing the limit of +5 per cent per annum from 1997 to 2002, while in China it was more than 10 per cent. Its share of jobs also stagnated at 17 per cent in the first years of the 21st century as compared to more than 25 per cent in China. Paradoxically, job-creation in the services sector also slowed down from 2.8 to 2.2 per cent per annum from 1983 to 1993 and from 1993 to 2000 in spite of a faster growth moving from 6.5 to 8 per cent. This concentrated growth of skilled jobs is due in a large measure to the lack of vigour of the mass domestic demand as well as supply constraints related to problems of governance, lack of adequate infrastructure and inflexible labour laws governing the principal organized sector. It is further aggravated by marked regional inequalities.

Table 4.3. Sector-wise Evolution of Employment 1983-1999

	1983	*1993*	*1999*	*1983*	*1993*	*1999*
		in millions		*in per cent*		
Agriculture	151	191	191	63	60	57
Industry and Construction:	37	50	59	16	16	18
Manufacturing	28	35	41	12	11	12
Construction	7	11	15	3	3	4
Services:	51	75	87	21	24	26
Trade, Hotels & Restaurants	18	27	38	8	9	11
Transport & Communication	7	10	14	3	3	4
Finance	2	3	5	1	1	1
Social and Personal Services	24	35	31	10	11	9
Total	**240**	**316**	**337**	**100**	**100**	**100**
Non-agriculture	*88*	*125*	*146*	*37*	*40*	*43*

Source : Planning Commission 2002 from NSS Surveys, based on Current Daily Status (CDS).

Table 4.4. Evolution of Labor Productivity in Selected Countries: 1960-2000 (yearly average growth per cent)

	60-70	70-80	80-90	90-00
Industrialised countries	4.1	2.1	1.5	1.5
East-Asia incl China	4.2	4.1	4.2	4.0
China	1.7	2.8	6.9	8.9
Latin America	2.4	1.7	-1.7	0.8
India	1.9	0.8	3.9	3.2
Middle-east	1.9	0.7	-0.5	0.0
Africa	4.6	3.5	1.8	1.2

Source: Borsworth and Collins 2003 in Rodrick and Subramanian [2004].

Geographically Concentrated Growth

Studies conducted during the last few years on India's spatial development, and particularly on the impact of economic reforms implemented since the 1980s [Bhattacharya, 2004], are all agreed on the marked unevenness of spatial growth together with an easily identifiable statistical dualism between the two halves of the Indian population as a whole. On the one hand, growth and development are restricted to only ten odd states and 3 Union territories, namely Delhi, Goa and Pondicherry. This India, according to some estimates, accounts for slightly more than half the Indian population and two thirds of its GDP, while its most active centres record an average growth of 8 to10 per cent per annum [Boillot, 2004]. As far as these "movers" are concerned, the convergence of some 40 socio-economic indicators highlights four main zones. Three of them form a very clear fertile crescent inclined towards the west: the South, and especially the Chennai- Bangalore stretch, which is more and more open to international trade, the hub of the National Capital Region around Delhi which tends to influence the entire north-west region and, finally, the Mumbai-Pune-Goa triangle which has the advantage of being in a strategic position in the middle of the fertile crescent and of its standing as India's financial centre opening out more to the mid-east. The dynamic hubs of Ahmedabad in Gujarat and Hyderabad in Andhra Pradesh are also closely connected to this fertile crescent. The more isolated eastern zone, consisting of West Bengal and the mineral-rich states of Orissa, Jharkhand and Chhattisgarh which had been regressing for a long time, seems to have woken up since the early 1990s. On the other hand, there is a central backward belt and small peripheral states whose average per capita growth is less than 2 per cent per annum. India also has to bear the burden of a prolific population growth in areas like the famous BIMARU states of Bihar, Madhya Pradesh, Rajasthan and Uttar Pradesh which account for 42 per cent of its population and a little over 50 per cent of its poor.

It so happens that this dualism almost amounts to a dichotomy between the coastal areas which are the most advanced and the interior, with the notable exception of Delhi, which may be compared to the dichotomy in China between the coastal provinces and the inland areas. The difference is that India is a big peninsula surrounded by the sea on three sides and not a dragon leaping into the ocean. That the National Capital Region (NCR) around Delhi, though situated far inland from the geographic viewpoint, is a part of the dynamic group of states, confirms that being away from the sea is more of a psychological than a physical drawback linked to traditional transport costs that are so important in economic geography. Delhi, which from the 11th century onwards was the capital of the invaders coming from the steppes of Central Asia and then from 1912 of the powerful British Empire in India (though India came under the British crown in1858, Calcutta, which was the headquarters of the East India Company, remained the capital until 1912), finally provided a sanctuary to the refugees of the Partition in 1947. It is now one of the most open areas of India and is fast becoming the nerve-centre of not only political but also economic power. Accounting for 3.1 per cent of India's GDP and with an annual growth of 8.9 per cent, it overtook its rival, Bombay, in 2003-04 with a per capita GDP of Rs.51,664 as compared to the national average of Rs.20,862.

One of the explanations for this apparent dualism between inland and coastal areas may be found in the works of Amartya Sen and his colleague Jean Drèze [2002]. All the socio-demographic indices for states, and even districts, show that there is a strong correlation between economic and social progress and the speed of demographic transition, which itself is conditioned by human development indicators dependent on prevailing socio-political structures. The regions lagging behind seem to have the most conservative and unfavourable social structures and, consequently, their human development indices trail behind other regions, especially in the domain of education, child nutrition and gender equality. Hence, when it comes to life expectancy, Kerala crossed the level of 70 years way back in 1990 while in the BIMARU states it is still below 60 years. Infant mortality has fallen substantially after the massive efforts undertaken by the Indian government in the 1980s through mass vaccination campaigns and the control of diarrheic diseases which are very common in India. But it was still 67 per 100,000 in 2002 which led UNDP to remark that it was a "South Asian enigma" accounting for 34 per cent of child deaths in the world with one out of fifteen children dying before the age of five. It is closely linked with malnutrition which affects 21 per cent of the total population, while 30 per cent of children below the age of 5 are underweight according to international norms. But gender inequality is supposed to be responsible for this situation as India holds the world record for anaemia among women explaining the high rate of death during child-birth (0.54 per cent). This phenomenon, which is prevalent in poor states where there is a marked inequality between castes, becomes even more evident when Kerala is compared with Madhya Pradesh where 13.8 per cent children die before they reach the age of five against only 2 per cent in the former. In more general terms, these inequalities in the field of health are followed by inequalities in education where the public education system leaves much to be desired and the lack of doctors in poor rural areas because private practice in urban areas is becoming an increasingly lucrative activity. In fact, healthcare facilities in Indian metropolises are now sought after by patients from all over the world who come to India for surgeries that cost three to five times less than in developed countries.

This explains the strong tendency that will be visible during the next twenty years: India, which is now marching ahead, will have one of the lowest fertility rates (the rate in South India is already comparable to that of developed countries), but it must reckon with the backward masses in the "Hindi Belt" which will account for the major portion (about 500 million inhabitants) of India's population growth during the next fifty years, particularly Uttar Pradesh and Bihar whose population is likely to rise from respectively 175 and 110 million to 320 and almost 200 million by 2050.

Unequal Growth in the Social Sphere

Measuring these inequalities with the help of the Gini coefficient of per capita expenditure apparently shows a relatively low level as compared to international levels and a great stability since 1950. From 0.337 in rural areas and 0.40 in urban areas, it has gone up respectively to 0.306 and 0.365 in 1997, or an average of 0.325 as compared to 0.546 in Mexico or 0.591 in Brazil, two countries which are typical of highly non-egalitarian societies. In China too inequalities increased significantly during the 1990s with an index of 0.447 according to UNDP [2004]. Actually, this stability is quite deceptive. The distribution of income does not take into account the significant shift of influence at all levels in favour of the new middle class which has really played a decisive role in the reorientation of the Indian economic model towards globalisation and consumerism. Besides, a more precise measurement shows that some of the inequalities increased during the 1990s [Banerjee et Piketty, 2003]. The share of income of households in the richest percentile thus increased from a low of 5 per cent in the early 1980s to 11 per cent in 1997 while the richest 20 per cent accounted for almost 42 per cent of the income as compared to barely 9 per cent for the poorest 20 per cent.

The comparison with China is equally instructive. Ravallion [2004] shows that in both countries, even though the economic growth brought down the level of absolute poverty during the 1990s, there was an identical decline in the distribution of the fruits of growth (coefficient of 0.63 as compared to equal distribution taken as 1). The difference is that the average annual increase of 6.2 per cent of the per capita income in China permitted a pro-poor growth of 3.9 per cent while it was only 0.8 per cent in India. The Chinese profile thus shows a minimum growth rate of about 3 per cent for the poor which moved up systematically to reach 9 per cent for the richest segment. In India, the graph seems more egalitarian but at the cost of a difference in growth with China which is decreasing only in the richest segment. India thus needs to accelerate its growth and also ensure that its benefits are spread more equitably among its population if it wants to reduce its level of absolute poverty faster and expand its domestic market for the benefit its traditional industries. But as most realistic writers admit, this would undoubtedly demand a radically different social structure [Varma, 2004]. In the meanwhile, India in banking on the trickle-down effect to come to the aid of its burgeoning middle class.

Table 4.5. State-wise Regional Disparities in India

	States Unite	*Population Million*	*GDP/capita* EUR PPP*	*GDP total* in EUR PPP*	*GDP/capita annual growth 2001/01*	*Agriculture % GDP*	*Industry % GDP*	*Services % GDP*	*FDI/ capita in INR*	*Bank deposits/ capita INR*
	INDIA	1037.9	1783	2047	2.4	27.77	23.21	49,02	2745	8215
1.	Andhra Pradesh	75.7	1748	147	5.6	31.51	21.51	46,98	1666	6682
2.	Arunachal Pradesh	1.1	1557	2	5.0	-	-	-	101	6315
3.	Assam	26.6	1117	33	1.4	41.00	21.86	37,14	1	3762
4.	Bihar	82.9	545	49	0.7	32.82	22.29	44,9	89	2989
5.	Jharkhand	26.9	0	0	NA	-	-	-	0	6457
6.	Goa	1..3	4815	7	-4.7	-	-	-	6549	54728
7.	Gujarat	70.0	2053	120	-0.4	17.97	36.80	45,22	2481	8148
8.	Haryana	21.1	2534	57	4.5	33.15	29.10	37,75	1520	9833
9.	Himachal Pradesh	6.1	2020	14	4.1	-	-	-	597	13100
10.	J & K	10.1	1324	15	0.0	33.84	16.53	49,64	8	4277
11.	Karnataka	52.7	1926	113	5.8	29.02	24.00	46,99	4024	8636
12.	Kerala	31.8	2078	74	4.4	24.29	22.03	53,68	465	10750
13.	Madhya Pradesh	60.4	1153	78	-11.9	35.00	26.10	38,9	1517	4821
14.	Chhattisgarh	20.8	0	0	NA	-	-	-	304	4054
15.	Maharashtra	96.8	2533	276	0.6	16.44	30.89	52,67	4909	13137
16.	Manipur	2.4	1369	4	-2.4	-	-	-	13	2123
17.	Meghalaya	2.3	1400	4	1.5	-	-	-	230	7780
18.	Mizoram	0.9	NA	NA	NA	-	-	-	17	3928

19. Nagaland	2.0	NA	NA	NA	-	-	-	19	4281
20. Orissa	36.7	912	39	-1.5	42.48	17.57	39,94	2242	4135
21. Punjab	24.3	2674	73	2.7	42.09	22.38	35,53	1842	19643
22. Rajasthan	56.5	1279	82	-8.8	31.60	26.39	42,02	469	4368
23. Sikkim	0.5	1660	1	NA	-	-	-	0	15426
24. Tamil Nadu	62.1	2123	147	3.5	17.96	29.01	53,03	3666	8636
25. Tripura	3.2	1532	5	5.1	-	-	-	2	4372
26. Uttar Pradesh	166.1	1038	193	1.5	37.27	23.31	39,42	279	5020
27. West Bengal	80.2	1716	150	4.8	37.81	19.00	43,19	1085	7852
28. A & N islands	0.4	NA	NA	NA	-	-	-	387	12837
29. Chandigarh	0.9	4739	4	1.8	-	-	-	1633	75389
30. Dadra & Nagar Haveli	0.2	NA	NA	0.0	-	-	-	5635	10455
31. Daman and Diu	0.2	NA	NA	0.0	-	-	-	3495	31456
32. Delhi	13.8	4149	61	0.5	-	-	-	24093	67416
33. Lakshadweep	0.1	NA	NA	0.0	-	-	-	83	11167
34. Pondicherry	1.0	3347	4	-1.0	-	-	-	12754	16516

Sources: CSO & various Official Surveys.

*Author's estimates computed with the average PPP conversion rate provided by IMF.

Table 4.6. Annual Income Distribution according to Class of Household

	*'000 INR**		*in current Euro*		*in PPP**		*Thousand Households*	
	1993-1994	*1997-1998*	*1993-1994*	*1997-1998*	*1993-1994*	*1997-1998*	*1997-1998*	*2006-07p***
The Very Rich	215.0	400.0	5923	9709	28430	46602	1.2	5
The Consumer class	130.0	241.5	3581	5862	17190	28136	32.0	75
The Rising Class	33.5	61.5	923	1493	4430	7165	55.0	82
The Poor	19.0	35.0	523	850	2512	4078	45.0	20
The Very Poor	16.0	30.0	441	728	2116	3495	33.0	17
Total No. of Households						166.2	199	
*Exchange Rate INR/Euro**		*36.3*	*41.2*	*4.8*	*4.8*			

Source: La structure de la consommation en Inde, ME de Bombay, Janvier 2003 (from various NCAER surveys); euro conversion by the author.

* From the conversion rate provided by IMF.

Box: Chapter 4 – Use of Microfinance as a Weapon to Combat Poverty

It is estimated that almost 300 million Indians are outside the purview of the traditional banking system. 70 per cent of the rural population have no bank accounts and almost 90 per cent have no access to bank loans. Due to the lack of access to facilities offered by modern financial institutions, only 0.4 per cent of rural households are covered by life insurance while only 0.2 per cent have crop insurance. Despite the inadequacies of the traditional banking system, there is nonetheless a growing demand for credit in India as evidenced by the rapid growth of microfinance institutions (MFI) and their clients: according to estimates, 50 to 75 million poor households, of which 40 to 60 million in rural areas, represent the annual need for credit amounting to approximately € 23 billion or 5 per cent of India's GDP, while € 170 million were disbursed during the financial year 2002-03. This lack of access to credit also affects small enterprises and only 37 out of 145 million have access to the services of traditional financial institutions, while 80 per cent of the110 millions farms continue to be small and marginalised.

But new experiments conducted on an increasing scale by NGOs as well as dynamic new private sector banks like ICICI show that microfinance could eventually prove to be a profitable instrument and particularly effective in the fight against poverty caused by economic exclusion. It covers the credit requirements of approximately 12 to 15 million poor households and it is estimated that the number of potential clients in India would amount to 50 to 75 million households. The number of borrowers' groups known as Self Help Groups (SHG) has gone up by more than 64 per cent per annum during the last four years and in 2004 there were approximately 800,000 SHG linked to the Indian banking system for loans amounting to about € 690 million. This remarkable phenomenon confirms the success of Bangladesh's longer experience in this area (Grameen Bank) where the rate of loan recovery is almost 95 per cent.

The myth of the great Indian middle class goes along with the myth of a "Shining India". There are however tangible signs that the domestic market has expanded to cover new social strata and that, in spite of its present income structure, there is a strong possibility that India's growth will eventually benefit all the strata of its society, even though not to the same extent as in China. The studies conducted regularly by NCAER (National Council of Applied Economic Research) distinguish five income groups among the 166 million households in India in 1997-98. The very rich comprise 1.2 million households whose number could rise to 5 million in 2006-07. A well-to-do class of consumers is estimated to include 32 million households whose number could well rise to 75 million in 2006-07. Finally, there is an upwardly mobile class of 55 million households whose number could reach 82 million in 2006-07. The middle class in a wider sense would, according to NCAER, rise from 14 per cent to almost 40 per cent of households, or 450 million persons in 2006-07. However, there were poor households (45 million) and very poor households (33 million) still comprising more than half the population in 1997-98 and NCAER expects their number to dip to about 37 million in 2006-07, but on the optimistic assumption that there will be an annual growth of 8 per cent. Up to now, the real middle class in the consumerist sense of the term consists of approximately 200-250 million persons having access to basic durable goods like television. Only half of them really have an income that would permit them to indulge in a western type of consumption (at domestic prices) while the rich number about 25 million [Bertrand 2003]. These large numbers are confirmed by consumption data. Thus the annual sales of cars went up from 300,000 in 1995 to almost 1 million in 2004, and the monthly sales of mobile telephone connections are about 2.5 million with the total number of subscribers exceeding 65 million in September 2005 as compared to 15 million in the beginning of the decade (but more than 350 million in China in 2005). Conversely, the stagnation of bicycle sales as opposed to the rapid expansion of the sale of twowheelers and the even faster growth of private cars reflects a marked inequality in the access to consumption which is causing much concern among Indian industrial groups like Bajaj and Godrej. The latter, more focused on the domestic market than on the international market, insists on the potential of the rural market and demands a sustained economic policy for the development of rural areas. They have won their case to some extent with the support of powerful regional parties, particularly due to government policies subsidising the agricultural sector and social programmes like the Employment Guarantee Scheme (EGS) enacted by the national Parliament in autumn 2005.

4.3. Can India Accelerate its Growth and Reduce Poverty?

The reduction of poverty depends on two factors as already indicated by François Bourguignon [2003]: vigorous growth and a change in the distribution of its fruits. With a per capita growth of 3 per cent per annum and a poverty rate of 20 per cent, it would take at least 10 years to reduce it by three fourths if the Gini coefficient changes from 0.55 to 0.45, but 30 years if there is no change. Indian planners are trying to act on both levels.

As regards growth, the results of the Tenth Five-year Plan (2002-07), which is now nearing its end, are quite disappointing. As compared to its initial goal of an annual growth of 8 per cent, Indian economy remains closer to 6.5 per cent in spite of a record growth of 8.5 per cent in 2003-04. However, the study carried out by Dani Rodrik and Arvind Subramanian [2004] shows that a growth of at least 7 per cent is quite possible during the period 2005-2025. The first favourable factor is the ratio between savings and investment. It has grown very slowly so far and is presently much lower than it was in most other Asian economies when they took off: for instance, 26 per cent of the GDP in India as compared to more than 40 per cent in China. But by 2025, the demographic equation will bring down the dependence ratio (inactive population : active population) from 0.62 in 2000 to 0.48 in 2025. This 14 point gain could lead to a mechanical rise in the savings rate taking it from 25 to 39 per cent of the GDP as generally observed during periods of demographic transition. Without any change in the net external contribution (a conservative assumption if you take into account the present growth of FDI), the supply of capital would rise by 8.3 per cent per annum as compared to hardly 6 per cent at present contributing on its own to a growth of 5.4 per cent per annum, keeping in mind an already substantial gain of 2.5 per cent in the total productivity of various factors. As for the contribution of human capital, the active population should increase by 1.9 per cent per annum during the next 20 years. With the same participation rate and level of education, the contribution of the labour factor would be 1.3 per cent taking the growth rate to 6.7 per cent per annum, or a per capita growth of 5.3 per cent against 3.6 per cent during the 1980-1990 decade.

This minimum rate will be boosted by some accelerating factors. As far as productivity is concerned, statistical regressions indicate that India could increase it by 30 to 40 per cent to catch up with its potential and that is exactly what the reforms undertaken during the last several years are aiming at. In terms of institutions, a comparison by the same writers with other emerging countries shows that the per capita income could actually be 4 to 5 times higher than it is at present if you take into account the stable democratic government, the efficacy of the rule of law and the respect of ownership rights. Further, from this point of view, the same regressions reveal a situation that is just the opposite of that prevailing in China whose economic performance has surpassed its institutional potential. The record stability of the Indian economy as compared to all the other emerging countries is in any case a well recognized fact.

A whole set of factors could however thwart this objective of accelerating economic growth and reducing poverty. There is always a possibility that the expansion of information technology may produce unexpected results and impede widespread development due to social or spatial constraints. At the social level, there is a risk that mass education may not spread due to caste barriers and that the spread of primary education may be slow among the poorest segments. At the geographical level, the spatial inequalities mentioned earlier must be taken into account. The most backward Indian states lack dynamic centres with a concentration of services and modern industries in spite of being the most dynamic areas from the demographic viewpoint. There is thus a strong risk of dualism and it could impede growth if the economic policy cannot successfully ensure its spread to all areas. This can be done through education and the development of infrastructure, that is to say public goods that only the state can provide or at least promote. So, given the present lack of proper governance [Jalan, 2005] and the risk of a limited growth of just 6 per cent, the possibility that poverty will be reduced in 30 years instead of 10 cannot be ruled out. Similarly, the fiscal tension between the central and state governments has intensified since the mid-1990s. With the accumulated deficit of the public sector being slightly above 10 per cent of the GDP, the financing of public investments is going down at the cost of debt-servicing and current expenditure. The near-crisis situation in the country's finances is cushioned by a mechanism of taxing domestic savings through a largely public-sector banking system and distorted banking rules.

But this is happening at the cost of productive investment and especially of credit for the productive small-scale sector. India's fiscal structure suffers from an excessively low level of tax collection even at the present level of development (between 12 and 15 per cent of the GDP) revealing the archaic structure of its tax-collection machinery as aptly pointed out in the famous Kelkar Report in 2004. On this point, India is committed to bringing about a real change during the coming years and the introduction of VAT in 2005 is a good sign. But the challenge is still formidable and determines the future of public investments, especially in the fields of education, health and basic infrastructure like the modernisation of the banking sector in a country where the banking network is still not effective in rural areas.

5

India and Globalisation

Although India was exposed very early in its history to maritime trade and later to colonial trade, after its independence in 1947 it adopted a very inward-looking and protectionist policy which reduced its share of the world trade to less than 0.4 per cent in the 1970s while its exports plummeted to only 3.5 per cent of its GDP. The presence of foreign companies in India was less than marginal, especially after the expulsion of multinationals like IBM and Coca-Cola by George Fernandes in 1977. The changes that occurred in the 1980s, and particularly in 1991, marked India's return to the world economic stage, and though the process was gradual in the early stages it picked up momentum as the years went by. Thus within a decade, India's share of the world trade rose to almost 1 per cent, being even more in the services sector which was responsible for the silent revolution in its balance of payments position. Structurally deficient since Independence, India was now financed by large invisible surpluses and financial flows following the gradual liberalisation of its capital account. For the first time in its history, its foreign exchange reserves were comfortable (US$ 145 billion in mid-2005) and permitted it to adopt a more offensive posture on the world stage.

5.1. Liberalisation in the 1990s

As for the goods trade, the measures taken in July 1991 put an end to import licenses for practically all goods except consumer goods. These licenses would disappear progressively towards the end of the Uruguay Round Agreements in April 2001 with a final notification in February 2002 regarding 715 products. Protection in the form of customs duties was also drastically reduced from 1993 onwards. Consequently, the peak customs tariff fell from 400 per cent in 1990 to 35 per cent in 2000 and 20 per cent in the 2005 budget while the average consolidated duty dropped from 72.5 per cent in 1990 to a little less than 30 per cent in 2005 (taking into account some additional taxes). However, this dismantling of the tariff structure had to face its share of resistance. India used all the regulatory tools at its disposal to slow down the effective opening up of its market, particularly anti-dumping measures, the first of which appeared in 1993. Since then, India has overtaken the United States as the first user of this instrument with almost 400 cases filed in 2005, about 20 per cent of which are against the European Union and about the same against China, and almost half of them pertain to the chemical industry [WTO, TPR Review, 2004]. As regards tariffs, agriculture is still highly protected (it still exceeds 50 per cent of the consolidated average) together with consumer goods (close to 60 per cent). Other industrial goods either carry a zero duty like electronics, because India encourages the import of electronic equipment at low prices to give a boost to its services sector, or around 10 to 15 per cent.

In the services sector, protection traditionally assumes the form of regulatory policies. Liberalisation was delayed because of the predominant role of the public sector until the early years of the 21st century. In December 1999, the law regulating insurance (IRDA) timidly opened up this sector by allowing foreign direct investment (FDI) up to 26 per cent while introducing strict regulations to ensure that the funds collected by insurance companies were invested in infrastructure and social sectors. In the banking sector, FDI was first allowed up to a level of 49 per cent and then 74 per cent in 2004, but under fairly restrictive conditions such as a 10 per cent cap on voting rights for each block of shareholders. Similarly, compliance with the commitments made at Marrakech has been postponed to 2009 with the Reserve Bank of India (RBI) following an ad hoc policy in the interim. The inevitable liberalisation of this sector explains the presence of 25 fully functioning foreign banks and more than 150 subsidiaries of foreign banks having a share of slightly more than 6 per cent of domestic bank credit. In fact, the RBI expects public sector banks to restructure themselves by 2009 and private Indian banks to reach a critical size like ICICI, the country's second largest bank after the State Bank of India (SBI).

Liberalisation of the infrastructure sector started at the same gradual pace with cent per cent liberalization in some segments like roads, ports and airports (decision taken in 2005). The real failure was in the energy sector due to the bungling of the Dabhol power generation project in 1998. However, the Electricity Act of 2003 proposed the total restructuring of the sector based on the classical separation between generation, transmission and distribution with the possible entry of foreign investors, while some private Indian companies have already taken over power distribution in Delhi. The successful liberalisation of telecommunications has effectively demonstrated that liberalisation can produce far-reaching and positive results. From being a state monopoly till the early 1990s, the telecommunications sector was thrown open to competition following the National Telecommunications Policy of 1994, even though the temptation to form cartels is still strong. Once the liberalisation process was completed in 1999, a powerful regulatory body (TRAI) was set up and FDI was permitted to the extent of 49 per cent as a first step and then increased to 79 per cent in 2005, and even 100 per cent for some Internet Services. As a result of this liberalisation, the number of mobile phone subscribers rose to almost 70 million towards the end of 2005 and the tariffs are among the lowest in the world.

This gradual liberalisation applied to all types of FDI. The automatic licensing procedure introduced in 1991 defined a long list of negative items including the classical sectors like defence, tobacco and alcohol, as well as those reserved for small and medium enterprises (more than 24 per cent of the capital). It also fixed the upper limit for participation, for example 51 per cent of the capital in 48 branches constituting the core of the manufacturing sector. The limit of 74 per cent, corresponding to the absolute majority for strategic decisions, was also continued in the case of eight branches including services, the mining industry and the bulk of the building industry. Even more controversial was the rule requiring joint ventures with Indian partners to obtain the latter's consent for starting a new project. Efforts to liberalise FDI had to put up with a series of objections raised year after year. Since 2005, permission is required only if it is a different type of activity, but from 2007 foreign companies will be spared the humiliation of being dictated to by their Indian partners. Officially, the new regime, which took charge in 2004, tried hard to speed up the liberalisation of FDI, especially as a compensation for the increasing number of acquisitions by Indian companies in other countries (cf. infra). But like the banking sector, it has come up against a whole lot of vested interests, as in the case of distribution and the insistence that liberalization should follow the direction dictated by India's interests and open up markets in developed countries for its manufacturing and services sectors.

Table 5.1. Comparison of the International Exposition between India and China 1980-2003

Million USD	*1980*	*1990*	*2000*	*2003*
Exports				
India	8,441	17,813	42,624	60,793
China	18,139	62,760	249,195	438,250
China+Hong-Kong	37,859	144,904	451,185	662,124
Imports				
India	14,822	23,991	50,336	69,827
China	19,505	53,809	224,942	412,836
China+Hong-Kong	41,904	136,291	438,261	645,381
% World Exports				
India	0.5 %	0.5 %	0.7 %	0.8 %
China	1.0 %	1.9 %	3.9 %	5.8 %
China+Hong-Kong	2.1 %	4.3 %	7.1 %	8.8 %
% World Imports				
India	0,8 %	0.7 %	0.8 %	0.9 %
China	1.1 %	1.6 %	3.5 %	5.5 %
China+Hong-Kong	2.3 %	4.0 %	6.9 %	8.6 %

Openess (X+M/GDP %)				
India	13.3 %	13.4 %	20.2 %	22.5 %
China	12.5 %	30.1 %	43.9 %	60.3 %
China+Hong-Kong	24.2 %	60.7 %	71.4 %	83.3 %

Source: WTO 2005.

Liberalising Capital Flows and the Dirty Trinity

Paradoxically, the liberalisation of capital flows was faster than the liberalisation of FDI. As compared to China, which is more liberal towards FDI but still very restrictive in the case of stock-market investments and loans in foreign exchange or in local currency, India successfully put to test the formula of investments by non-resident Indians (NRI) during the foreign exchange crisis in 1980. The liberalisation of investments by foreign institutional investors was took place in the 1990s under the close supervision of RBI and a special regulatory authority – SEBI – was set up in 1995 to monitor stock market operations. Recently, foreign institutional investors have even been allowed to cover up to 30 per cent of their risk in foreign exchange. The result of these measures is the continuous increase in the flow of foreign capital attracted by the view that Indian has a strong growth potential and by confidence in the market's legal security. Stock market investments reached a record of net flows worth US$ 10 billion in 2004 as compared to US$ 5 billion in the case of FDI. A welcome development was the very comfortable position of foreign exchange reserves in 2005 together with a stable external debt which enabled the government to relax regulations controlling the outward flow of capital as Indian companies are increasingly attracted by investments abroad and need funds to finance cheaper imports. From 2003, no permission was required to buy foreign exchange amounting to 50 per cent of the net value of acquisitions abroad. In the case of mutual funds keen on diversifying their portfolios, the ceiling on investments abroad was raised to US$ 1 billion in 2003. Finally, conditions for commercial loans for Indian companies were substantially relaxed in 2004 in order to spare the RBI the high cost of controlling the entry of foreign funds. In all, the balance of payments surplus rose to US$ 20 billion in 2004, or the same amount as the trade deficit. Did this mean that India ran a greater risk of facing a financial crisis like many emerging countries?

These liberalisation measures were part of a gradual and prudent reform of the exchange control regulations governing the Indian rupee. Following directions from the IMF, the latter became convertible for current account operations only in August 1994. This partial convertibility was later extended to capital accounts. But the RBI wanted to maintain a strict control over the competitiveness of exchange rates as well as inflation, two variables which have been very sensitive all through India's economic history. The result of this was a "dirty trinity", a reference to Mundell's famous incompatibility theorem which proved that it is not possible to have at the same time a fixed or stable exchange rate, an independent monetary policy and a free circulation of capital. Keeping these three objectives in view, India has adopted an intermediate monetary regime that is neither completely flexible nor based on a fixed exchange rate. The rupee's partial convertibility allows it to make continuous adjustments between its goal of containing internal inflation, which compels it to play with interest rates and the money mass in circulation, while maintaining its exchange rates at a fairly competitive level to ensure the medium-term equilibrium of its balance of payments. The lessons learnt from the Asian crisis in 1997 have given rise to a strong consensus in the country against the premature liberalisation of the rupee.

Table 5.2. Balance of Payments of India 1990-2004 (bn USD)

	1990/91	*2001/02*	*2002/03*	*2004/05p*
Current account Balance	**-9.7**	**3.4**	**6.3**	**2.5**
Merchandise Trade Balance	-9.4	-11.6	-10.7	-23.6
Merchandise Exports	18.5	44.7	53.8	81.4
Merchandise Imports	27.9	56.3	64.5	105.0
Balance of Non-factor Services of which:	0	3.3	3.6	9.5
Software Services		7.6	9,.6	*15.5*
Net Income	-3.8	-4.2	-3.4	-4.6
Net Transfers	3.5	15.9	16.8	21.2

Capital Account Balance	7.2	8.6	10.8	20.4
Net Direct Investment	0.1	4.7	3.2	5.3
Net Portfolio Investment	0	2.0	0.9	9.9
Net External Assistance	2.2	1.1	-3.1	2.1
Net Commercial Borrowings	2.2	-1.6	-1.7	0.5
Net Short-term Credit	1.1	-0.8	1.0	1.1
Net NRI Deposits	1.6	2.8	3.0	-1.2
Foreign Exchange Reserves	**5.8**	**54.7**	**76.1**	**136.8**
In months of next year's imports (g & s)	*1.5*	*8.0*	*9.3*	*10.9*
	313	474	497	580

Source: RBI and IMF 2005.

5.2. India Still a Commercial Dwarf though Slowly gaining Prominence

It is still too early to say whether India's liberalisation will produce the same overall results as China's. The similarity of their pace of development has been verified at one level. In India, the ratio of the trade in goods and services almost doubled during the first decade of liberalisation rising from 17 to 31 per cent of the GDP between 1990 and 2000 as compared to the rise from 18 to 34 per cent in China, one decade earlier. As the observed annual growth continued at a pace of 15 to 20 per cent per annum, the distortion continued at the same pace with the liberalisation rate reaching 34 per cent of the GDP in 2004 and expected to approach of 40 per cent towards the end of the decade. India's is trying to increase its pace of liberalization in an effort to catch up with other Asian economies as it is still at the bottom rung of the liberalisation index calculated by the international research institute CEPII for its foreign trade weighted by the GDP measured in terms of purchasing power parity: India's 9.8 per cent against Pakistan's 16.4 per cent, China's 21.6 per cent and Thailand's 50.5 per cent [Chauvin & Lemoine, 2003]. A theoretical model used by IMF established in 2002 that the volume of trade between 1995 and 1998 was 70 to 80 per cent lower than the country's theoretical potential, keeping in mind its GDP and its geographical location. At the same time, a World Bank study demonstrated that India's trade regime was one of the most protectionist regimes after Cameroon and

Pakistan with an average weighted tariff of 29.5 per cent for imports (1999) and 32.3 per cent for just manufactured goods as compared to respectively 15.7 and 14.7 per cent in China. As regards the trade in goods, India's return to the world stage continues to be very gradual. While China's share (including Hong Kong) of the world trade in goods went up from 2.1 to 4.3 per cent between 1980 and 1990 and soared to 8.8 per cent in 2003, India's share stagnated at 0.5 per cent during the first phase to rise to just 0.8 per cent in 2003. At this stage, the ambitious target of 3.5 per cent of world exports set for 2015 seems reachable even though it will still be lower than France's share (5.2 per cent) today.

But apart from this dualistic image of a commercial dwarf in the process of catching up rapidly with other countries, what needs to be questioned is the idea of a simple time-lag in relation to China since the two models present a totally different set of structural features. There are undoubtedly indications of a time-lag such as a more protectionist trade policy, a liberalisation rate that is twice as slow and a much lower growth dynamic that is responsible for a gap of 1:2 in their respective GDPs, all of which automatically explains the importance of the two Asian giants in world trade. To these gaps must be added the various structural differences that can explain why there is a real difference of 1:6 or even 1:9 if we include Hong Kong. The first factor concerns the relative importance of the industrial sector in the GDP which is much lower in India than in China: 27 per cent against 49 per cent. If the services sector is taken into account, there is a significant change in the perception of India's liberalisation as it represents one third of India's exports. The second factor concerns the very different nature of FDI in the two economies.

Foreign Direct Investment (FDI)

Liberalisation of FDI seems to be one of the major factors responsible for the vast difference between the two Asian giants and the ratio of 1:10 is frequently mentioned in the UNCTAD data base (US$ 55 billion in China in

2004 and only US$ 5.5 billion in India). But the classical image conveyed by such a big quantitative difference is rather simplistic because it is technically wrong and overlooks the originality of the Indian globalisation model. In the first place, the data cannot be compared. An in-depth study by Srivastava in 2003 shows that India does not follow the IMF methodology as it refuses to include stock-market investments of more than 10 per cent of the capital or the reinvestment of profits, which would amount to US$ 8 billion of FDI in 2001 instead of the 3 billion recorded officially. Further, China has a tendency to overestimate its FDI with the famous "round-tripping" of Chinese funds coming through Hong Kong to take advantage of tax benefits and other less commendable practices. After these deductions, it would appear that the real FDI in China was no more than US$ 20 billion in 2000. The second difference is the optical illusion produced by the two economies according to which China's GDP is twice as much as India's. However, corrected data show that the real FDI constituted 1.7 per cent of the GDP in India as compared to 2 per cent in China. As a matter of fact, the presence of foreign goods is equally visible, perhaps even more so in India. Half the leaders in the big consumer markets are foreign brands, except for some basic consumer goods. The third difference is the rate of investment, which is 1:2 or slightly more than 20 per cent of the GDP in India and almost 40 per cent in China. Paradoxically, FDI plays a relatively more important role in India and its economists incessantly question the rationality of the Chinese rate of investment being so high for such a small difference in their respective growth and could give rise to the assumption that capital is being used more rationally in India.

If we take into account the nature of FDI and the direction of growth, we find that multinational companies have a tendency to go in for heavy investments in technology and capital-intensive sectors, whereas more than half the FDI in China is directed towards labour-intensive sectors, particularly funds coming from non-resident Chinese of Hong Kong, Taiwan and Singapore who launched an-export-driven growth strategy way back in the 1960s. In fact, the ratio of FDI to exports is virtually the same in the two countries and illustrates the bias in China's export-driven growth strategy. On the other hand, FDI by major multinational companies represented no more than US$ 4 billion in China ten years after its liberalization in 1980 and 13 billion in 1997. FDI flows having reached an annual rate of US$ 5 to 8 billion, and Prime Minister Manmohan Singh having fixed a target of US$ 150 billion for 2015, India could easily catch up with the China's FDI which is essentially domestic. Besides, is it not possible that following its steep rise, India's IT services sector could take the place of China's export-driven manufacturing sector?

Table 5.3. FDI Inflows into India 1980-2004: % Domestic Capital Formation in billion USD

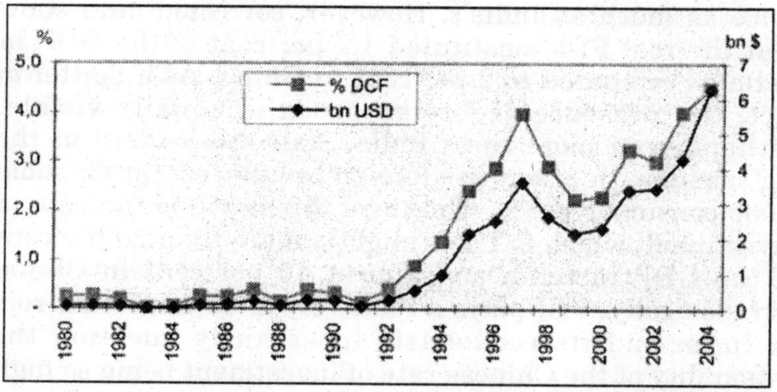

The Upswing of IT Services

India's breakthrough in the international services sector is a fairly recent phenomenon. With an annual growth of 17 per cent during the 1990s as compared to the world average of 5.6 per cent, India became the world number one due to the dynamism and the importance of the services it exported. These exports rose from 2 to 5 per cent of India's GDP between 1995 and 2005. Focusing mainly on information technology (IT) and business process outsourcing (BPO), in 2004 these exports generated an income close to US$ 20 billion to which may be added the almost 8 billion brought in by experts working on fairly long projects abroad, or about one third of the income from the export of goods. The history of the IT sector goes back to the early 1980s when the present giants, Infosys and Wipro, were set up by engineers who had gained valuable experience in the United States, side by side with TCS (Tata group). Their return to India was facilitated by a policy supported by Nasscom and the technical ministries concerned which set up technology parks (STP) centred around the Indian Institutes of Technology (IIT) and various government agencies involved in scientific research like DRDO (defence), C-DAC (information technology) and C-DOT (telecommunications). These parks enjoy various tax benefits including duty-free imports of the latest equipment. Attracted by this dynamic setup, companies all over the world started investing directly in India or outsourcing their software operations and gradually other services like accounts and, increasingly, services involving communication with clients through the famous "call centres". The latest entrant is Knowledge Process Outsourcing (KPO) covering pharmaceuticals, biotechnology, legal and medical services and even R&D, and its total turnover is expected to go up to US$ 17 billion by 2010. According to Nasscom estimates, the international outsourcing market for just litigation support to American lawyers was US$ 5 billion in 2005.

Having been recognised as a country with a strong growth potential, foreign investments in India rose rapidly in this sector by 36 per cent per annum all through the 1990s and represent nearly a quarter of the country's total FDI today. The top 20 Indian companies in this sector still account for half its turnover with the Tata company, TCS, taking the lead while foreign multinationals (GE, Cap Gemini etc.) account for a little less than a quarter of the exports. In 2000, at least 160 of the 500 world class companies listed by Fortune magazine had outsourced a part of their software operations to India. Their number rose to about 400 in 2005. To this must be added a hundred odd multinationals which have set up R&D

centres in India and their list is becoming longer as ten or so are added every month. In all, India receives almost 40 per cent of the IT projects meant for developing countries, followed by China (19 per cent) and Singapore (11 per cent) where there is a considerable Indian presence. If multinationals are now acquiring sick Indian companies [UNCTAD, 2004], Indian groups themselves are going global by buying specialised companies all over the world, particularly in Europe, or setting up branches in their principal markets today (68 per cent in USA) or in future markets (China and the Asia-Pacific region being their special targets). More than 300 Indian companies are thus present in the United States and almost a hundred in Europe, the second largest software market in the world.

As a result, Indian exports of actual IT services shot up from US$ 0.5 billion to 15.5 billion in 2004 and they aim to reach a turnover of 100 billion in 2008 of which 50 billion will be for the export of software, 30 billion for the domestic market and 20 billion for the electronic industry itself. To this will be added other services provided to companies, or what are known as "IT-enabled services", whose exports rose from 0.6 billion in 1999 to close to 5 billion in 2004, of which 58 per cent for multinationals like American Express, British Airways and HSBC. According to the consulting firm McKinsey, India's share of the global "off-shore" market in these two branches amounted to 25 per cent in 2001 (since then it has overtaken Ireland), but it was 67 per cent for just "IT-enabled services".

5.3 Geographical Changes: The "Look East" Policy

The change in India's trade policy corresponds to a structural shift in the world economy in Asia's favour. The new economic geography progressively taking shape gives us an idea of the new pattern of world trade that will emerge during the coming decades. In 1990, the European Union, then consisting of 15 countries, was by far India's largest trading partner accounting for 29.1 per cent of its exports and 33.7 per cent of its imports. The former USSR slipped from the second to the third place in India's exports (15.7 per cent) but still maintains a marginal place in its imports (3.6 per cent) due to the long distance to be covered for transporting oil and gas from the Middle East. Its place was taken by North America during the 1980s as India's second largest export market (16.9 per cent), with imports at the same level. In fact, from one end to the other, Asia (mainly Japan + Newly Industrialised Countries) already occupied the second place among India's export markets even in 1980, after the European Union. China's rapid rise as a trading power during the 1990s, together with the liberalisation of the Indian market, hastened this important shift in India's trading pattern in favour of Asia and particularly China.

Table 5.4. Sectoral Structure of India's Foreign Trade (% of total)

	1980	1985	1990	1995	2001
Textiles	28.0	23.5	31.6	32.5	30.1
Food and Agriculture	34.2	27.5	21.1	18.4	15.8
Chemicals	6.2	5.7	9.3	11.3	14.7
N.E.S.	8.1	10.1	14.7	15.2	14.4
Machinery	7.2	5.7	6.0	5.2	6.4
Iron and Steel	7.7	6.3	5.3	5.6	4.7
Energy	0.9	15.7	5.5	3.0	3.6
Electrical	1.7	1.3	1.3	1.4	2.5
Wood and Paper	1.5	0.8	0.9	1.7	2.3
Electronic	0.7	1.0	1.6	1.8	2.2
Vehicles	2.6	1.3	1.7	2.5	1.9
Non-ferrous	1.2	1.1	1.2	1.5	1.4
Total	100	100	100	100	100
	1980	**1985**	**1990**	**1995**	**2001**
Energy	42.4	24.4	25.7	21.6	27.7
Chemicals	13.7	18.3	15.2	16.8	15.1
N.E.S.	3.8	6.1	11.8	11.4	11.8
Machinery	13.1	17.9	17.4	18.7	11.2
Electronic	2.7	6.1	6.2	7.1	8.8
Food and Agriculture	8.3	8.8	4.8	5.9	7.6
Non-ferrous	4.1	2.9	3.2	3.3	4.1
Wood and Paper	2.0	3.0	3.1	3.1	3.8
Electrical	1.8	2.5	2.6	4.0	3.3
Iron and Steel	6.4	7.1	7.1	5.1	3.2
Textiles	0.5	0.9	1.4	1.6	2.2
Vehicles	1.3	1.9	1.4	1.5	1.2
Total	100	100	100	100	100

* *Mostly gems* and *jewellery.*

Source: CHAUVIN S., LEMOINE F. [2003], CEPII CHELEM Database.

US –EU: Relative Decline of Strategic Stakes

The European Union's share of the Indian market declined by half, falling to 18 per cent in 2003. India's export outlets in the European Union showed more resistance, but eventually its exports fell to about 21 per cent. Finally, the EU had a trade surplus of barely € 1 billion in 2004 considering that India's exports were now increasing faster than its imports. What is important from the EU's point of view is that India has become a very marginal partner accounting for just 1.7 per cent of its total trade (with all the 25 members) in 2004. The relative intensity of trade has also decreased since the mid-1990s to a level closer to 1 during the last few years, that is to say a level strictly comparable to the importance of the two entities in the world, while it was close to 1.6 in 1990. The exceedingly traditional composition of India's exports, dominated mainly by labour-intensive goods and raw materials, largely explains this change with reference to the expansion of this trade towards East Asia in the early 1990s as well as its preference for countries of the Mediterranean rim. However, the decline in Europe's share in India's market also means that Europe has become less competitive and lacks dynamism as compared to Asia and even the United States.

The latter manages its geo-economics quite efficiently in accordance with the new post-Cold War geopolitics. India is fast acquiring a strategic position on this new geopolitical map together with China, Central Asia and the Middle-East. However, the loss of the contract for the sale of 54 Airbus planes to Boeing in May 2005 shows how much pressure is exerted on India by the United States whose goods exports to India were only 6 per cent as compared to almost 30 per cent during the period 1960-1970. From Europe's viewpoint, this is more important than the erosion of its trade with India. Conversely, the role played by the American market in India's exports definitely increased during the 1990s overtaking EU15 in 2002, even more so because we must take into account the export of IT services satisfying the needs of two thirds of the American market as compared to only a quarter of the EU market. The result is a substantial increase in India's presence in the American market even though it is still barely 2 per cent as compared to China's 18 per cent, thus leaving a sizeable margin for future readjustment. As in China's case, the United States' negotiating power can now bank on a gaping deficit in their bilateral trade which reached US$ 4 billion in the goods sector and close to 10 billion in the services sector. However, the United States can offer as compensation 80 per cent of the temporary work permits (H1B Visa) to Indian software professionals. Added to its position as the largest foreign investor in India, equal to Europe, and the preferred destination of Indian overseas students (whose number is larger than Chinese students), the redeployment of American strategy in India's favour amounts to a conjunction of geo-economics and geopolitics at a time when India has accepted the challenge of globalisation and is prepared to negotiate the terms for its rapid entry into the world of superpowers. In contrast, Europe's relative economic decline, which is not backed by any active geopolitical considerations in the subcontinent, has changed the balance of power to the point of making it a more or less a silent partner vis-à-vis the tripolar world of 2020-2050 comprising the US, China and India as projected by one of the influential institutes in New Delhi [Virmani, 2004b].

Table 5.5. Changing Pattern of the Geographical Distribution of India's Foreign Trade since 1960

EXPORT	1960-61	1970-71	1980-81	1990-91	2000-01	2003-04
OECD	66.1	50.1	46.6	53.5	52.7	46.4
EU15	36.2	18.4	21.6	27.5	22.7	21.1
USA	16.0	13.5	11.1	14.7	20.9	18.0
Japan	5.5	13.3	8.9	9.3	4.0	2.7
OPEC	4.1	6.4	11.1	5.6	10.9	15.0
ex-USSR	4.5	13.7	18.3	16.1	2.0	1.1
Dev Countries	14.8	19.8	19.2	16.8	26.7	32.6
Africa	6.3	8.4	5.2	2.1	3.2	3.3
Asia including	6.9	10.8	13.4	14.3	21.4	27.6
China+HK**			0.7	0.8	4.6	7.3
Latin America	1.6	0.7	0.5	0.4	2.1	1.7
Others	8.0	2.7	1.0	6.2	7.3	4.2
Total	**100**	**100**	**100**	**100**	**100**	**100**

IMPORT	1960-61	1970-71	1980-81	1990-91	2000-01	2003-04
OECD	**78.0**	**63.8**	**45.7**	**54.0**	**39.9**	**37.8**
EU15	37.1	19.6	21.0	29.4	19.8	17.3
USA	29.2	27.7	12.9	12.1	6.0	6.4
Japan	5.4	5.1	6.0	7.5	3.6	3.4
OPEC	**4.6**	**7.7**	**27.8**	**16.3**	**5.4**	**7.2**
ex-USSR	1.4	6.5	8.1	5.9	1.0	1.2
Dev Countries	**11.8**	**14.6**	**15.7**	**18.4**	**17.5**	**20.1**
Africa	5.6	10.4	1.6	2.2	1.7	1.3
Asia including	5.7	3.3	11.4	14.0	14.4	17.2
China+HK**			2.3	3.2	7.9	9.5
Latin America	0.4	1.0	2.5	2.3	1.5	1.5
Others	**2.2**	**0.4**	**0.5**	**3.5**	**36.0**	**33.3**
Total	**100**	**100**	**100**	**100**	**100**	**100**

Sources : Indian Customs, IMF DOTS (calendar years).

The New "Look East" Policy

The shift towards Asia clearly picked up speed during the 1990s. From just about 12 per cent in 1960, India's exports rose to 23.6 per cent in 1990 and reached 35.3 per cent in 2003, making it the principal zone of attraction for Indian trade. With a comparable volume of imports, with the exception of oil, East Asia has become the new centre of gravity for an India trying to restructure and intensify its relations through a more offensive trade policy involving a large number of bilateral and regional free-trade agreements. The latter are meant to expand India's export market in a fast developing area where its presence is still quite marginal and to counterbalance China's growing importance in trade in an East Asia which hopes to get the world's second largest demographic power to join the regional game to neutralize China's increasing influence.

The notable trait of India's relationship with these Asian partners is the relative decline of Japan and the stagnation of Korea and Taiwan as compared to China + Hong Kong. Japan's share of the Indian market thus dropped from 10.6 per cent in 1980 to 7.5 per cent in 1990 and 3 per cent in 2004. Korea's share, which rose steeply during the 1990s, suffered a real downturn in the beginning of the 21st century and plummeted to 2.8 per cent. Conversely, in 2004 the China-Hong Kong combine claimed the largest share of exports to India amounting to almost 10 per cent of the total, and even more if you take into account the non-official flow of goods coming in through neighbouring countries or even Dubai and Singapore, the real nerve centres of the trade in cheap Chinese goods. Even if you take just mainland China, the monthly turnover has crossed US$ 1 billion, or the annual total three years earlier. The aim is to raise it to US$ 30 billion by 2010, considering that the current rate of trade is 2.5 times lower than the theoretical potential calculated with the help of gravitational models. In spite of a strong upswing in the 1990s, the relative intensity of the trade is still less than 1 for the two partners.

This change is the result of the conjunction of two structural effects. On the one hand, the rapid growth of the two Asian giants and the simultaneous liberalisation of their trade have automatically driven them to better each other. This effect can be measured by the growth in each partner's imports in terms of their GDP: from 0.2 per cent for both in 1990, to 0.6 per cent for China and 1 per cent for India in 2003. On the other hand, the sectoral specialisation of each giant during this first phase of the upswing showed a rare complementarity between the two countries so similar in size and level of development. On India's side, the relative decline in the share of most industrialised countries in its market is in fact only a reflection of China's transformation into a world manufacturing centre where Japanese, Korean and even American and European companies have congregated to engage in the mass and low-cost production of consumer goods like mobile telephones (Nokia, Motorola, etc.) household appliances and office equipment (80 per cent of the world's photocopiers) as well as textiles and toys sold all over the world. Apart from the numerous Chinese companies that survive by dumping enormous quantities of goods requiring little technology, there are cheap copies of well-known brands in the "China Bazaars" of developing countries. On the Chinese side, the main imports from

India are intermediate products like steel, iron ore (two thirds of its world exports), basic chemicals and synthetic yarn since its production capacity and raw materials which cannot keep pace with the demand. Manufactured goods as such occupy a marginal place. But what is remarkable is that India, which has traditionally suffered from an inferiority complex due to China's over-competitiveness, has for several years had a surplus balance as far as the official trade is concerned, which triggered the "Chindia" campaign at the end of 2004 targeting China as India's strategic partner during the coming years in both geopolitics and geoeconomics [CLSA 2005 and Ramesh 2005]. Is this likely to happen?

India-China, International Centre of Gravity or Rivalry?

It is necessary to be cautious and look beyond the automatic impulse that drives each of these two countries to adapt itself to the growing export market represented by the other. While economic pragmatism may be at the root of the Realpolitik that led to the convergence of these two giants aspiring to become world powers and the warming of their diplomatic relations 42 years after the 1962 conflict, the same economic and political dynamics could give rise to as many rivalries as potential complementarities. Firstly, because of the lessons taught by the theory of big markets and the very different demographic dynamics that will appear during the coming decades when India will become younger and China will grow older from 2015 onwards. India's advantage in this respect, together with its aggressive reforms policy, further corroborates the theory of the emergence of a second China in South Asia. This is what companies all over the world are beginning to establish by targeting India as the world's second manufacturing and services centre to reduce the risk of an excessive dependence on China while continuing to profit from a market perceived as having a mediumterm potential. The opening of a production and R & D centre by Nokia in India in 2005 is but one instance among the dozens of similar projects announced every month.

Further, because of the substantial difference in their present strength. At the economic level, their GDP is not equally matched, China's GDP being 2.5 higher than India's while the gap between them is 1:10 in world trade; on the bilateral level, the actual flow of goods into the subcontinent during the last few years reveals a fast growing bilateral deficit visà- vis China. Besides, when China's new capacities for the production of intermediate goods – set up during the massive investment cycle between 1997 and 2005 – come into operation in the near future, they could pose a threat to India's exports, especially steel and plastics and, even worse, push up Chinese exports of these very same goods leading to a lowering of prices in the Indian market as already witnessed in 2005. When the yuan sneezes, the rupee gets a cold and not vice-versa. China gave India a real shock when textiles quotas were lifted in 2005 leading to a small but unexpected fall in India's exports which made the Indian government and industrialists ponder seriously on the situation.

Finally, on the political level, China is a recognised nuclear power and a permanent member of the United Nations Security Council armed with the veto. Its opposition to Japan's entry into the Security Council by blocking the initiative of the Group of 4 which includes India, may be no more than a timely action at a time when it was launching a major offensive to seduce the entire subcontinent. Similarly, India's new trade diplomacy with East Asia and other countries of the sub-continent could be just another indication of a reasoning based as much on competition as on the complementarity between the two Asian population giants.

Pakistan's Thorny Record and SAARC

Paradoxically, India is experiencing the greatest difficulty in building a relationship with its immediate neighbours based regional economic integration in the place of the geopolitical obstructions that have built up since India's partition in 1947, not only in relation to Pakistan but also Bangladesh whom it helped attain independence in 1971. The intraregional trade officially constitutes just about 5 per cent of the total trade of the five main countries of the subcontinent (to which must be added the informal trade estimated at US$ 1.5 billion between Pakistan and India as compared to the official flow of US$ 250 million). A South Asian Association for Regional Cooperation (SAARC) was nonetheless established in December 1985 under the leadership of India's new Prime Minister, Rajiv Gandhi, who was determined to combine politics with economic reforms while ushering in a new era of peace with his neighbours – Bangladesh, Bhutan, Maldives, Nepal, Pakistan and Sri Lanka. But it was only during the 7th SAARC Summit in 1993 that the seven member countries signed the first agreement liberalising the trade between them, namely the South Asian Preferential Trade Agreement (SAPTA), with the avowed aim of setting up a free-trade zone by 2001. The Indo-Pakistan confrontation in Kargil in 1999 followed by the nuclear tests by the two neighbours, postponed the date to 2008 and 2010 during the SAARC Summit in 2000.

The sudden change in the geopolitical situation following the attacks on New York's World Trade Centre on 11 September 2001 brought about a change of attitude in Pakistan whose black decade in the 1990s made it realise that its policy of military confrontation with India would only lead to an economic impasse. India on its part was becoming increasingly aware of the fact that an unstable neighbourhood could prove to be a stumbling block in its efforts to become a 21st century world economic power. Even though bilateral relations with Sri Lanka, Maldives, Bhutan and Nepal made considerable progress from the mid-1980s, its two immediate neighbours on either side, Pakistan and Bangladesh, posed problems. The subsequent warming up of relations with Pakistan made it possible to relaunch regional negotiations during the historic Islamabad Summit in January 2004 where the seven SAARC countries signed a framework agreement to bring down to zero the customs duties on almost all the goods traded by members by 2016. If things had progressed as anticipated, SAPTA should have made way for SAFTA from January 2006. The most developed countries (India, Pakistan and Sri Lanka) should bring down their customs tariffs to less than 20 per cent by the end of 2007 and then to zero during the five following years, while the least developed countries will be given three extra years to accomplish this.

There is no doubt that everything depends on the continuation of good political relations with Pakistan and a substantial advance in the resolution of the Kashmir issue. The eastern border with Bangladesh is not very secure either because of the fragile political situation in that country. In Nepal, the King has recently been stripped of all his powers by a popular uprising led by the Maoists and supported by the political parties who are framing a new democratic constitution. It is becoming more and more evident to the economists of this region [RIS 2004] that one way of getting out of the regional vicious circle combining political instability and under-development is to use the economic lever in an area that still accounts for 40 per cent of the world's poor. While the population of the subcontinent is now higher than China's (1.4 billion as compared to 1.3 in 2003), its combined GDP is 2.5 times lower due to the fragmentation of national economies which gives rise to severe under-productivity. The most recent calculations of the trade potential by ICRIER show for example that India's trade with Pakistan could be US$ 7 to 13 billion more than the present level as compared to US$ 4.5 to 16 billion with China (depending on whether the calculations are based on the respective GDPs at current exchange rates or on purchasing power parity). In addition to the psychological effect that would reduce the region's risk premium, which is still quite high, the creation of an integrated regional economic zone would offer significant advantages in terms of specialization and exposure to the outside world, both for India and its neighbours. The best example would be security of energy supply through Pakistan (pipelines coming from Iran and Central Asia) and Bangladesh, which has substantial under-exploited gas reserves and which could also give permission for laying a gas pipeline from Myanmar. As far as Indian companies are concerned, the possibility of accessing a market of 350 million more consumers at their doorstep makes them ardent votaries of peace in South Asia. As regards the other countries rich in energy and agricultural raw materials and well known for their manufactured products like Pakistani textiles, access to a market of more than 1.1 billion consumers would certainly give a boost to industries suffering for neglect at present.

6
India, a New 21st Century Power?

India's great stability in the emerging world, thanks mainly to its democratic regime – even though far from perfect – lends itself rather well to economic projections, especially with two sets of structural parameters: demographic transition and the gradual pursuit of reforms first launched in the 1980s. Nevertheless, contrasting scenarios prove to be more productive in the context of some major uncertainties related to development strategies and the social and environmental challenges in the subcontinent that are as formidable as its size.

6.1. Forecast for 2025-2050

Demographic Window of Opportunity

The Indian demographic equation during the coming decades is perfectly compatible with the concept of the demographic window of opportunity that links the structural transformations produced by the existing demographic transition activating an economic virtuous circle, but only to the extent that the country's institutions and strategy permit it. The first transformation corresponds to the change in the rate of dependence that links potential savings with the number of inactive persons supported by the active population (inactive/ active ratio). The second relates to the availability of jobs and has a doubly stimulating effect since the number of active persons (15-59 age group) will grow faster than the total population together with a decrease in the average age of the active population that is expected to be healthier and better trained. The third set of transformations corresponds to the effects of the market. On the one hand, the Indian population will continue to increase, but at a slower pace, so that by 2030 it will overtake the Chinese population, which will then be about 1.4 billion, to reach the figure of 1.6 billion in 2050. On the other hand, this population will undergo major changes since the urban population will rise from 285 million in 1980 to 700 million in 2050 [Dyson et al., 2004], and the share of agriculture in India's GDP is likely to fall below 10 per cent in 2025. Theoretically, these effects when taken together cannot but stimulate demand factors by 6 to 8 per cent per annum. But, in that case, what about supply?

A Potential Growth of 6 to 8 per cent by 2025

Among the best known studies, two provide fairly accurate and credible estimates of India's potential growth during the coming decades in spite of using very different methodologies. The first of these studies, known by its famous acronym BRIC, standing for Brazil, Russia, India and China [Goldman Sachs, 2003], uses a conditional convergence model inspired by the theory of endogenous growth *à la* Barro. Potential growth is the result of a combination of internal permissive factors (investment rates, growth and education level of population and the quality of institutions), and the increase of productivity (technological convergence) boosted by the initial difference between India's per capita GDP and that of the most advanced country. In spite of an investment rate which will remain about 25 per cent of the GDP, and a mediocre education coefficient, the basic BRIC scenario indicates a potential growth rate of 5.8 per cent per annum during the next 30 years with one major phenomenon: the Chinese pace of growth will go into decline around 2010-15 and fall to +3 per cent per annum by 2040-50 against +5 per cent in India. A high variant admits a possible growth rate of even +7.4 per cent by 2030 with a faster convergence rate linked mainly to a large investment in education. The second study by Rodrick and Subramaniam [2004], already mentioned at length in

Chapter 4, is inspired by the same endogenous growth theory approach, but confined exclusively to internal parameters. It may be recalled that it considers a central scenario with a potential growth of 6 to 7 per cent per annum by 2025 or one point higher than the BRIC scenario that seems more indicative of a minimum growth. The BRIC scenario too contains a set of accelerating factors which would take India's growth close to the 8 per cent sought by its rulers. Thus the consensus seems to be a figure between 6 and 8 per cent during the coming decades.

Table 6.1. Comparative Demographics India and China 1950-2050

	Total Population in Million		*% world*		*annual change %**				*Dependency Ratio***	
					Total population		*15-59 years*			
	India	*China*	*India*	*China*	*India*	*China*	*India*	*China*	*India*	*China*
1950	358	555	14%	22%					73	61
1955	395	609	14%	22%	2.0	1.87	1.1	0.6	74	72
1960	442	657	15%	22%	2.3	1.53	2.0	1.0	76	78
1965	495	729	15%	22%	2.3	2.07	2.0	1.7	78	80
1970	555	831	15%	22%	2.3	2.61	2.2	2.9	79	79
1975	621	928	15%	23%	2.2	2.21	2.4	2.3	77	78
1980	689	999	16%	22%	2.1 1	48	2.5	2.8	74	67
1985	766	1 070	16%	22%	2.1	1.38	2.5	3.0	72	55
1990	849	1 155	16%	22%	2.1	1.53	2.4	2.2	69	50
1995	936	1 219	16%	21%	1.9	1.08	2.1	1.2	68	48
2000	1 021	1 274	17%	21%	1.8	0.88	2.2	1.2	64	46
2005	1 103	1 316	17%	20%	1.6	0.65	2.1	1.4	60	41
2010	1 183	1 355	17%	20%	1.4	0.58	1.9	0.7	55	38
2015	1 260	1 393	17%	19%	1.3	0.56	1.6	0.1	52	39
2020	1 332	1 424	18%	19%	1.1	0.44	1.3	-0.1	50	43
2025	1 395	1 441	18%	18%	0.9	0.24	1.1	-0.6	48	46
2030	1 449	1 446	18%	18%	0.8	0.07	0.8	-0.9	47	50
2035	1 494	1 443	18%	17%	0.6	-0.05	0.6	-0.8	46	55
2040	1 534	1 433	18%	16%	0.5	-0.13	0.4	-0.4	46	61
2045	1 568	1 417	18%	16%	0.4	-0.23	0.08	-0.6	47	63
2050	1 593	1 392	18%	15%	0.3	-0.35	-0.15	-1.0	50	65

Source: United Nations [2004].

* five-year average.

** Ratio inactive/active population (15-59 years).

6.2. Contrasting Alternative Scenarios

A team consisting of top Indian experts[1] spent several months in 2004-2005 with the World Economic Forum working on a more qualitative method of forecasting contrasting scenarios for 2025. The advantage of such a forecast is that it highlights both internal and external parameters that could act as real discriminating factors, not only in terms of growth rate but also the type of development that India should follow during the next twenty years in accordance with the strategy followed by the government as well as all the decision-makers in the public, political, social and business domains. They outlined three contrasting scenarios based on two trends: one, integration with the world economy or isolation from it and two, inclusive or exclusive growth.

The first scenario called "Bolly World", a pun on Bollywood, the name by which the flourishing Bombay film industry is popularly known, foresees a situation of excessive globalisation principally focused on information technology where growth is exclusive as it leaves out rural areas and unskilled labour. However, the rapid growth during the first phase is likely to flag after 2015 with the emergence of a less consensual society. The second scenario called "Atakta Bharat" (India getting stuck) evokes a mediocre international environment with very slow reforms, particularly in the field of infrastructure like water-supply and electricity, so that the gains of globalisation and increasing exclusion give rise to economic instability and bring back the "Hindu Growth Rate" of 4 per cent towards 2025. Finally, the third scenario called "Pahale India" (India First) tries to reconcile rapid international integration with inclusive growth, thanks to an active economic policy that reinvests the dividends of globalisation in voluntaristic programmes in the realms of health, education, antipoverty measures, physical

1. Including Sanjay Purohit, Development Director of Infosys, Rajiv Kumar, then Chief Economist of the Confederation of Indian Industries (CII), and Arun Maria, Chairman, Boston Consulting Group India.

infrastructure and, finally, good internal governance and good neighbourly relations with the immediate neighbours. Growth would remain quite high, even in a mediocre international environment (compensated by internal demand), and would even quicken after 2015 to reach the Chinese rate of 10 per cent per annum towards 2025. This set of scenarios thus presents a fairly wide bracket of growth ranging from 4 to 8 per cent and, what is more important, a very different picture of India's economic future that justifies the development of some crucial parameters like good governance in general, public investments in physical and social infrastructure and finally, a better wage structure.

6.3. Indian Economy and the World in 2025-50

Change in the World Population Scenario

Although its population will reach 1.6 billion in 2050, India's relative share of the world population will stabilise at about 18 per cent as it will have then entered the last phase of its demographic transition while Africa will still be midway. As a result, Africa's population will overtake India's in 2030 when it will be just above China's and soar to 2 billion in 2050 thus largely exceeding India's population at the end of the 21st century. Nonetheless, India is going to partially change the world's demographic equation for two reasons. Firstly, the rapid aging of the population of developed countries and even China will give India an unprecedented advantage in the world, excluding Africa. The population of Europe, including the former Soviet Union, will drop to one third of India's population while it was the world's largest population in 1950 equal to China's. The population of the United States will decline relatively slowly and fall below 5 per cent of the world population, while that of a highly developed Western Europe (excluding U.K.) will plunge to 2 per cent, like Japan's. On the other hand, the structure of India's population could give it an upper hand for a few decades because of the high proportion of active population. Africa, in addition to its uncertain politico-economic future, will have to bear the burden of a large under-15 population and thus have the highest dependency rate in the world until 2030, when the population of developed countries followed by China will start aging. Between 2030 and 2060-70, India could benefit from the lowest dependency rate in the world due to a good balance between the young and the old tilting in favour of the younger generation, including students and workers. It will thus represent almost 20 per cent of the world's youth (15-24 years) between 2015 and 2025, or twice the number in greater Europe and United States taken together, and the number of school-going children will no longer be in the ratio of 1:10 as in 1970 when there were as many young people in Europe as in India. As for the actual active population (15-59 years), India will probably overtake China in 2025 to end up with 250 million more active persons in 2050. According to UN projections, it will represent 70 per cent of the five-year variation at the world level in this age group during the next few years and will be well ahead of the rest of the developed world during the next half-century.

It is however advisable not to be carried away by the euphoria of the Indian government and media who tend to confuse demographic transition with economic transition. The challenge posed by a high active population is not peculiar to India. In China, the notion of a "potential" active population conceals a rural transition which means that for several years there will be a high demand for modern jobs from the rural population. The urban Chinese work force could thus rise from 250 to 350 million between 2005 and 2025 against 109 to 187 million in India, while the 15-59 age group will begin to decline in China towards 2015 and will subsequently fall by 10 million per annum between 2020 and 2050. Rather than India "taking over" from China, during the coming decades, the two Asian giants will dominate the world labour market and many other domains. This is all the more likely since between 2020 and 2050 Africa may take over from India as the biggest potential supplier of workers in the active age group even though their employability appears rather doubtful today.

Table 6.2. India-China : Structural Changes in Population 1990-2005 and Forecast up to 2025

	Population aged 15-59 in Millions		*Total employed Population**		*of which Urban***	
	India	*China*	*India*	*China*	*India*	*China*
1990	481	736	293	652	68	175
1995	534	783	331	690	79	200
2000	596	830	340	720	62	225
2005	662	890	393	770	109	250
2010	728	922	430	796	136	275
2015	788	924	466	799	154	300
2020	840	918	498	793	171	325
2025	886	893	522	773	187	350

* Current daily status for India

Sources: UN Population Division and author's estimates for 2005-25

A Gradual Return to the World's Economic Summit

Despite its numerous limitations and conceptual flaws, the BRIC scenario draws attention to the importance of economic inertia in spite of the major demographic changes in the world. As regards the masses, it is useful to compare the GDP of the two countries measured in terms of parity of purchasing power (PPP) to get an idea of the enormous size of the potential market.[2] From this point of view, India already ranks fifth after the USA, the European Union taken as a whole, China and Japan [IMF, 2005]. Its growth at the rate of 6 per cent per annum during the next 30 years can only be considered as an important incentive for the world economy and raise India's relative share even higher so that it reaches the combined share of EU-25 in 2030 and the combined share of EU and USA in 2050. China's GDP is however likely to be approximately 20 per cent more than India's in terms of PPP. But on a per capita basis, it should be noted that though this assessment in terms on PPP may appear

2. The PPP compares countries according to the domestic prices of equivalent products and not the market exchange rate of their currencies which expresses the relative level of productivity/competitiveness of goods and services traded in the international market.

favourable, the difference in the domestic standard of living will continue to be 80 per cent as compared to Europe (France, in this case) in 2025 and 60 per cent even in 2050.

But what matters most for any consumer is solvency and for any producer productivity. It therefore follows that to determine the change in a country's economic weight, it is necessary to take into account the market value of its currency, the so-called current exchange rate. And that is exactly what the experts from Goldman Sachs have done using econometric tools for their forecast, with two lessons to be drawn from the tables given below.

First, India's total GDP on the basis of the prevailing exchange rate is likely to be only one third of China's GDP in 2025, if we take into account China's present lead and the difference in the growth rate that was quite low to start with. From this point of view, the assumption that India will take over from China appears too simplistic. In 2050, India may reduce the gap by half, but it would still have a handicap of about 40 per cent equal to half of USA's GDP. Although we may wish to avoid a comparison with China regarding a future that is sometimes considered uncertain, it cannot be denied that the possibility of India having a GDP almost equal to that of EU-15 in 2050 or 20 per cent less than that of the United States will constitute a significant change in the world economic scene in 50 years time. Further, the process is not likely to be linear. In 2025, India will still be far behind the United States and Europe and will have just overtaken Germany. Given the selfcongratulatory stance adopted by some Indian elites regarding India's status as a superpower by 2025 and also the alarm this sometimes raises in the West, the time factor seems to be quite important to permit a positive sum game withthese new-comers and the implementation of the necessary adjustment strategies.

Secondly, what is actually more informative is the per capita GDP which paints a disappointing picture of the country's relative productivity. According to the optimistic BRIC projections, India's per capita GDP would be only US$ 2,330 in 2025, or ten years behind China's and ten times lower than that of France in 2000. In 2050, the difference between India's and China's per capita GDP would continue (a paradoxical effect of the decrease in China's population) and it would be 60-70 years behind that of France. This reality conveyed by figures highlights India's sluggish progress as well as the slow decline of its population and justifies the voluntaristic outlook of the Indian government desirous of maintaining the same pace of growth and globalization in the sectors in which the country is discovering its capabilities. India's and China's emergence as economic powers indicates that changes are taking place at the international level, two of which can be pointed out here.

Table 6.3. India in the World Economy 2005-2050: the Goldman Sachs BRIC Projections

Total GDP in PPP in bn USD (at 2000 prices)						
	India	*China*	*France*	*EUR4**	*Japan*	*USA*
2005	3299	7323	1702	7298	3687	11413
2010	4440	10319	1856	7457	3829	11744
2015	5920	13666	2023	7598	4044	12049
2020	7796	17425	2209	7732	4344	12350
2025	10295	21735	2399	7868	4629	12659
2030	13764	26520	2594	8002	4836	12963
2035	18559	32018	2800	8143	4894	13261
2040	24813	38656	3059	8287	5023	13553
2045	32583	45911	3321	8433	5232	13851
2050	42022	52862	3613	8580	5543	14142
Total GDP at market exchange rate (at 2000 prices)						
2005	604	1724	1489	6424	4427	11697
2010	929	2998	1622	7047	4601	13271
2015	1411	4754	1767	7689	4858	14786
2020	2104	7070	1930	8292	5221	16415
2025	3174	10213	2095	8780	5567	18340
2030	4935	14312	2267	9284	5810	20833
2035	7854	19605	2445	9957	5882	23828
2040	12367	26439	2668	10804	6039	27229
2045	18847	34799	2898	11687	6297	30956
2050	27803	44453	3148	12594	6673	35165

GDP per capita, in USD at market exchange rate (at 2000 prices)						
2005	559	1324	24547	24554,7192	34744	39552
2010	804	2233	26314	26763,01103	36172	42926
2015	1149	3428	28338	29104,94853	38626	45835
2020	1622	4965	30723	31371,67085	42359	48849
2025	2331	7051	33203	33284,6231	46391	52450
2030	3473	9809	35876	35376,93548	49944	57263
2035	5327	13434	38779	38266,04172	52313	63017
2040	8124	18209	42601	42014,45784	55721	69431
2045	12046	24192	46795	46135,69767	60454	76228
2050	17366	31357	51594	50582,99681	66805	83710

Source: Goldman Sachs [2003].

6.4. Accompanying Changes

Impact of the Increasing Outsourcing of Services on the World Labour Market

The unprecedented progress of China's manufacturing industry has unnerved many countries and instead of adopting a constructive attitude they are only too ready to accept defeat. The ongoing technology revolution in the services sector has made services tradable goods all over the world, even health-care services where the cost difference justifies long-distance travel by patients. WTO experts estimate that the trade in services could catch up with the trade in goods by 2050 at the latest and India is busy preparing itself for this change. But what will be the magnitude of this impact and how soon will it be felt?

According to a report prepared by McKinsey [2005], it is technically possible today to transfer offshore 11 per cent or 41 million jobs in the sector providing services to enterprises in developed countries. However, by 2008 a whole set of economic factors or factors related to learning and experience would reduce the demand for international outsourcing of services to only 4.1 million jobs against 1.5 million in 2003, or barely 1 per cent of the present jobs in the services sector of developed countries. On the supply side, the stock of young qualified professionals in low-wage countries would theoretically be 33 million, but the actual figure will be closer to 3.9 million considering the barriers of language and experience (7 years of experience is generally required), of which 25 per cent will be in India against only 10 per cent in China and 50 per cent in Hungary, where the population is much smaller. Conversely, the stock of young professionals in the eight leading developed countries included in the study would be 15 million out of which 8.8 million would be available for outsourcing by international firms. Taking into account the difference in the average hourly cost which would be 1:10 in the United States, there would be pressure for a rise in wages in low-cost countries. This is exactly what India is worried about (+30 per cent per year in 2004 and 2005).

Though circumstances are changing, the supply of qualified young professionals is rising at the rate of just 1 per cent per annum in the industrialized countries against 5 per cent in others. India in particular is following an aggressive strategy in the field of advanced training. In 2015 it expects to have 15 to 18 million students and produce 1.4 million engineers every year as compared to 350,000 at present and 50,000 PhDs against 19,000 in 2005. The present increase in salaries has led to an increased supply of training facilities in the private sector which will exceed by 50 per cent the total number of seats available in the field of higher education as most of the leading teaching institutes of the world are planning to set up branches in India which offers a very lucrative market. Of course, India is not the only country as there was a drop of 25 to 30 per cent in the salaries of qualified young professionals in China in 2004 following an unprecedented rise in their numbers. But India already produces 5 million graduates every year and, according to McKinsey, the cost of salaries is expected to remain the most attractive (after the Philippines) even in 2008, and demographic projections for the 15-24 age group are particularly favourable. Following the success of efforts in the field of education in both India and in China, it appears that the internationalisation of services is likely to assume almost "Chinese" dimensions during the next few years and move rapidly up the value-added chain towards R&D. Cost-saving and reaching a critical mass in terms of the domestic market and pool of researchers are particularly crucial in R & D since this is where the cost is the highest in industrialised countries. As the last

UNCTAD report published in 2005 points out, the possibility of China emerging as a new R&D hub is not so bright since Indian companies have a longer experience in this field and are used to working in a market economy. Because of this, they are determined to increase their supply even in other activities not covered by the McKinsey report like legal and medical services. Finally, they are very serious about globalisation and had already set up 35 branches in China itself in 2005, which they believe will be the second international centre for sourcing during the coming years, together with the prospect of the present US$ 25 billion domestic market growing at the rate of 30 per cent per year.

Impact on the World Energy Map

In 2004, the world realised to what extent China was influencing the world oil market because, even though it accounts for only 8 per cent of world consumption, it represents 40 per cent of the marginal demand. India's situation is not so well known. Consuming a little less than half the quantity required by China, India is now the world's sixth largest oil consumer and the third in terms of marginal demand after China and the United States. Its consumption has gone up by a little over 6 per cent per annum during the last decade as compared to the world figure of +1.5 per cent. The high-speed development of its petrochemical industry with the ongoing construction of the world's biggest refinery (20 million tonnes) makes it one of the leading actors in the oil sector as evidenced by the growing number of acquisitions of oilfields by Indian companies in Africa and especially in the former Soviet Union together with strategic projects for laying pipelines from Iran, Central Asia and Myanmar at the possible cost of a strategic peace with Pakistan. As a matter of fact, India imports 75 per cent of its oil and its domestic production is slowly going down after having peaked at 32.4 million tonnes in 2000 while its total requirements are expected to be 150 million tonnes in 2008 making it the world's 4th largest consumer, 224 million tones in 2020 and almost 500 million tonnes in 2047 (average between the highest and lowest brackets) according to the Green India Report brought out by TERI [Pachauri, 2002].

During the next few years, energy will be a major impediment to India's progress and its mass effect could influence the entire geopolitical and geoeconomic landscape in this sector. Although it is already the world's sixth largest oil consumer, its per capita consumption is still one of the lowest in the world with the equivalent of 531 kg of oil (2001) against 896 in China, 4017 in Germany and 8080 in USA. Even though its radiant intensity can be substantially improved because, paradoxically, it is one of the least efficient in the world, the demand for energy is likely to increase in India from 455 to 722 billion TOE by 2012, by which date the Indian government would like to electrify every single home in the country. This target by itself represents an increased power generation of 100 billion kW in 8 years and it should triple by 2020 because at present only 20 per cent of Indian homes are supplied electricity in the normal manner with an average per capita consumption of 365 kwh per annum in 2001 as compared to 8351 in France and 3600 in Poland. But how can this be achieved? The Tenth Five-year Plan which intends to produce two thirds of the country's power from thermal sources expects that coal consumption will double to 538 or 688 million tonnes depending on whether circumstances are favourable (low growth of energy consumption) or normal, while the consumption of oil and gas will triple as compared to the present consumption rising respectively to 195-245 million tonnes and 65-70 billion cubic metres.

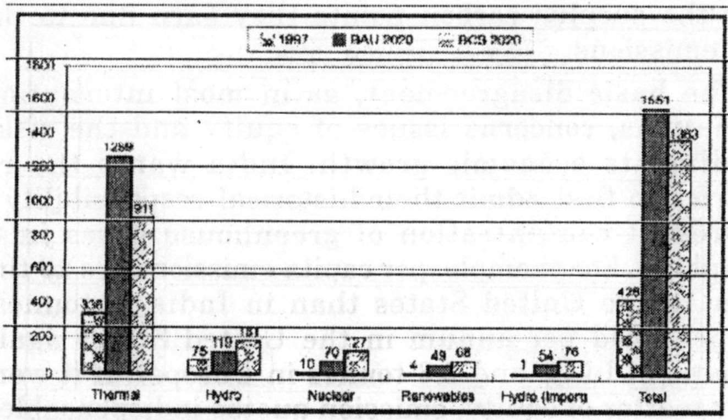

Table: Data Related to the Graph

Table 6.4. Official Forecast of India's Primary Energy Use for Electricity Generation in 2020 (in TWh)

	Thermal	Hydro	Nuclear	Renewables	Hydro (import)	Total
1997	336	75	10	4	1	426
BAU 2020	1259	119	70	49	54	1551
BCS 2020	911	181	127	68	76	1363

Source: Planning Commission [2002b]; BAU=Business as Usual; BCS=Best Case scenario.

Box: Chapter 6 – India and the Kyoto Protocol – An Ambiguous Position

Experts are of the view that India, which is presently ranked sixth in the world for its level of greenhouse gas emissions and second after China for the growth of emissions, will account for more the 10 per cent of the world's emissions by 2030. But at the same time, it also runs the risk of becoming one of main victims of these greenhouse gases because it faces severe problems of drought and uneven distribution of rainfall over time and space. This correlation should actually encourage it to participate very actively in the fight against global warming, particularly within the framework of the Kyoto Protocol signed in 1997. But that is not the case. Although India has signed the Protocol, it has not committed itself to reducing its emissions and has taken shelter under the so-called "flexibility" clauses that allow developing countries to enter into agreements with foreign companies to share the benefits of CO2 reduction by selling to the latter the surplus carbon points they earn due to their lower emissions.

The basic disagreement, as in most international negotiations, concerns issues of equity and the risk of impeding its economic growth. India wants the rich countries to first admit their historical responsibility for the present concentration of greenhouse gases in the atmosphere. For example, per capita emissions are 20 times higher in the United States than in India (6 tonnes of CO2 per head per annum in the United States against 0.3 tonne in India and 2.3 tonnes in Europe). If it were a purely matter of equity, emission quotas indispensable for reversing this trend would be allotted on a pro rata basis according to the number of inhabitants. On the contrary, the United States, which is not a signatory to the Kyoto Protocol, upholds the "grandfathering" clause and the principle of economic efficiency which should not subordinate economic growth to the necessity of reducing emissions. Since India fully concurs with the United States on this last point, it agreed to participate in the Vientiane Initiative in August 2005 involving six countries including China, Japan and Australia. The idea is to focus on technological solutions that are easily accessible to developing countries. Actually, India is hedging its bets and claims to be one of the countries most active in the joint implementation of the Kyoto Protocol for the introduction of Clean Development Mechanisms (CDM). In 2005, almost a hundred projects were submitted to the Indian national authority (DNA) in charge of approving these partnerships. It is evident that in the medium run the international community has to find compromise solutions that will permit India (as well as China) to control emissions in the future without compromising its economic progress.

Taking into account the probable change in the prices of hydrocarbons[3] and polluting emissions that are hardly compatible with the preoccupations of the international community (see box), India seems to be faced with a difficult choice. The share of hydroelectric power, already 17 per cent in 1997 with 75 TWh, is expected to go up to 19 per cent in 2020, but at the cost of increased imports from neighbouring countries (Bhutan and Nepal) which impose certain constraints due to geostrategic and geographical reasons (concentration of sources in the Himalayas). There are only two other alternatives: the first indicated in the Plan Report emphasizes the use of renewable sources of energy that will be significantly advantageous from the economic, social and environmental

3. The Planning Commission [2002b] mentioned in its 2002 report a price ranging from US$ 17 to 23 per barrel during the next 20 years, a price that hardly seemed economically viable.

viewpoints. In India, which is already the world's fifth largest producer of electricity, wind, sunlight and biomass are important potential sources of electricity that hold the promise of creating employment in rural areas. But as things stand at present, these alternate sources will represent hardly 5 to 10 per cent of the generation capacity in 2020 unless there is a major technological and economic breakthrough in the world. So the only other option left is nuclear energy and the controversy about its use has been reopened after the warming of Indo-US relations in 2005 followed by negotiations on a nuclear agreement between the two countries.

India has been pursuing nuclear research at an advanced level but the division between the military and civil uses of nuclear power has always been blurred, and this is what provoked the signatories of the Nuclear Nonproliferation Treaty to impose international sanctions against it after the second Pokhran explosion in 1998. Despite its isolation, India pursued its ambitious plan of increasing its civil production capacity from 3.3 to 20 GW by 2020 so that the share of nuclear power will rise from 2.5 to 6 per cent of the electricity produced with 15 reactors that are already installed and 9 others in the process of being built. The lack of self-sufficiency in uranium, the technical difficulties involved in building a thorium-based system, even though a quarter of the world's thorium reserves are located in India, and because it is uneconomical to produce energy from so many disparate sources, India has had to relegate nuclear energy to a marginal position in the absence of international cooperation. It is possible that the conjunction of economic considerations, the increasing pressure to lessen the shortage of power and, finally, the new geopolitical relationship with the United States and Europe (whose technological superiority in this field is recognized), could once again make nuclear energy the focus of attention, especially because of the medium-term scenario in relation to China, and bring back the international credibility India lost in the 1990s.

Conclusion

The emergence of India as a fast developing and dynamic economy is gradually replacing its traditional image of mass poverty. Apparently, conditions seem to be ripe for the country to pursue its rapid growth trajectory during the coming decades and take its place alongside China as one of the leading political and economic actors on the world stage. To achieve this, India will have to face enormous challenges as indicated by various prospective scenarios: governance, especially in the states whose population will be the same as that of the European Union comprising 15 countries; a drastic improvement of the infrastructure, particularly transport and power; social and environmental sustainability including an end of mass poverty; a rapid improvement in the education level in rural areas and, finally, controlling the overpopulation of megacities already suffering from severe water and housing problems. But even as things stand today and taking into account India's democratic regime, which despite its innumerable defects is still able to exert pressure on its decision-makers, there is nothing to indicate that India's efforts to transform itself will come to naught.

Seen through the eyes of the rest of the world, India's emergence on a level with China portends major changes fraught with risks but also great opportunities for which preparations should begin today itself so that it can learn to handle them effectively. There will be large-scale changes in terms of globalisation, particularly in the services sector in which India is indeed a pioneer, but the advent of totally new technologies should make the trade in services catch up with and then overtake the trade in goods. Another major challenge will be to safeguard the earth's environment in the face of the present struggle for black gold, the renewal of nuclear energy and the difficulties of associating these new powers with the Kyoto

Protocol on climate change; finally, there are geopolitical challenges related to these economic transformations with the opening of a new set of alliances involving India, especially with the United States which seems to have taken the initiative in 2004, but which cannot ignore Europe.

Basic Data regarding India and China in 2005*

		India	*China*
Demography and National Income			
Population	Millions	1105	1308
Population density	Pop/km²	318	134
Urban population	% to total	29	41
Net birth rate	per 1000	1.6	0.6
Life expectancy	Years	63	71
GDP	US$bn	773	2225
GDP - per capita	US$/person	700	1702
GDP (PPP)	US$tr	3633	9412
GDP - per capita (PPP)	US$/person	3288	7196
Share of GDP	%		
Agriculture	%	20.0	12.0
Industry	%	26.0	47.0
Services	%	54.0	40.0
GDP growth, historical 5Y avg	%	6.3	9.5
Expected GDP growth 2003	% Cagr	7.5	9.6
Household savings rate - Saving/GDP	% of GDP	24.0	11.6
Infrastructure			
Electricity production	bn kWh	614	2469
Electricity consumption - per capita	KWh	556	1885
Port handling capacity	million tonnes	287	1426
Rail routes	thousand km	63.7	67.5
Telephones - Fixed lines	per 1,000 people	123	570
Cellular phones	per 1,000 people	65	395
R&D expenditure	% of GNP	0.6	0.1
Motor vehicles	per 1,000 people	10	14
TV sets	per 1,000 people	104	416
Government			
Fiscal deficit /GDP - 2002 (1)	%	7.8	1.5
Total public debt /GDP - 2002 (1)	%	82	27
External sector			
Exports (including software)	US$bn	103	762.5
Imports	US$bn	158	628.4
Current acct (deficit) surplus as/GDP	%	-2.5	7.2
Forex reserves	US$bn	145	818.9
FDI inflow - 2002	US$bn	5.3	54
Non-resident remittances	US$bn (2001)	28	76.8
External debt/GDP	%	70	11
Capital market and banking			
Market capitalisation aug-2005	US$bn	620	428
Listed companies		5863	1200

Social sector			
Adult literacy	%	57	91
Education expenditure/GNP	%	2.9	2.5
No. of graduates per year	million	1.2	1.45
Internet users	million	20	110
Doctors	per 1,000 people	0.5	1.6
Health expenditure/GDP	%	6.1	5.8

* unless specified

Sources: World Bank [2005] and CLSA [2005]

BIBLIOGRAPHY

Useful Websites

Official information: www.gksoft.com/govt/en/in.html

General information about India: www.indiainfoline.com

Ministry of Finance: www.finmin.nic.in

Planning Commission: www.planningcommission.nic.in

Reserve Bank of India (RBI): www.rbi.org.in/

Indian confederation of Indian industry (CII): www.ciionline.org.

Demographic and Social data available on: www.censusindia.net.

Books and Articles

BATRA A. [2004], "India's Global Trade Potential: The Gravity Model Approach", ICRIER Working Paper No. 151, New Delhi.

BERTRAND X. [2003], La structure de la consommation en Inde, fiche de synthèse, Mission Economique de New Delhi, DGTPE, Paris.

BOILLOT J.J. [1985], Industrialisation et ouverture de l'Inde : 1950-1985, Economie Prospective Internationale, n°2, la Documentation Française.

BOILLOT J.J. [1988], Régulation et Développement, le modèle indien depuis 1947, Ph.D thesis, Univeristy of Paris X - Nanterre.

BOILLOT J.J. [1992], Le financement de l'industrialisation: Investissement, épargne, croissance, in La CHINE et l'INDE en transition, Numéro spécial Économie Prospective Internationale, N°50, 2è trimestre 1992, La Documentation Française.

BOILLOT J.J. et alii [2004], Analyse comparative des Etats et Territoires indiens, ed. Ubifrance, Paris, septembre 2004 (147 pages).

BOILLOT J.J., MICHELON N. [2001], Chine, Hong Kong et Taïwan, une nouvelle économie géographique de l'Asie, La Documentation Française, Paris. Also available in English on the website: http://www.cefc.com.

BOURGUIGNON, F. et PEREIRA da SILVA L., eds.[2003], The Impact of Economic Policies on Poverty and Income Distribution: Evaluation Techniques and Tools. Washington, D.C.: Oxford University Press and the World Bank.

CHAUVIN S., LEMOINE F. [2003], India in the World Economy: Traditional Specialisations and Technology Niches, CEPII Document de travail, No 2003 – 09 August.

CLSA [2005], CHINDIA, The Shape of Things to Come, Investment Strategy, Summer 2005.

DATT G., RAVALLION M. [2002], Is India's Economic Growth Leaving the Poor Behind?, Journal of Economic Perspectives, Volume 16, Number 3 - Summer 2002 - pp. 89-108.

DATT R. & SUNDHARAM K.P.M [2004], Indian Economy, 49th edition, S. Chand & Co., New Delhi.

DEBROY B. ed [2004], Agenda for Improving Governance, Academic Foundation in association with the Rajiv Gandhi Institute for Contemporary Studies, New Delhi.

DELEURY G. [1997], Gandhi, Pygmalion Gérard Watelet, Paris.

DEWAN-VERMA [2002], Slumming India, a Chronology of Slums and their Saviours, Penguin Books India.

DORIN B. (ed), FLAMANT N., LACHAIER P., VAUGIER-CHATTERJEE A. [2000], The Indian Entrepreneur, Manohar, New Delhi.

DORIN Bruno, LANDY Frédéric. Agriculture et alimentation de l'Inde, les vertes années [1947-2001]. INRA Editions. INRA Paris, 2002].

DUPONT V., TARLO E. et VIDAL D. eds. [2000], Delhi: Urban Space and Human Destinies CSH-Manohar, New Delhi.

DYSON, Tim, CASSEN R., VISARIA L. [eds.], Twenty-first Century India. Population, Economy, Human Development and the Environment. New Delhi: Oxford University Press, 2004. p. 414.

FRANKEL Francine: India's Political Economy (1947-1977), Princeton University Press, Princeton, 1978, 600 p.

GAIHA I. & N. [2005], Millennium Development Goal of Halving Poverty in Asia and the Pacific: Progress, Prospects and Priorities, Discussion Paper IFAD.

Goldman Sachs [2003], "Dreaming with BRICs: The Path to 2050", Wilson Dominic, Purushthaman Roopa: Global Economics Paper No. 99 1st October 2003.

GORDON J., GUPTA P. [2004], "Understanding India's Services Revolution", IMF Working Paper, WP/04/171.

GUILMOTO P. [2005], chapter on population in JAFFRELOT [2005a].

GURCHARAN DAS [2000], India Unbound, from Independance to the Global Information Age, Penguin Books India, New Delhi.

HUMBERT Philippe: Inde - Les années Rajiv Gandhi (1984-1989), L'Harmattan, 1990, 282 p.

IMF [2005], World Outlook, Washington D.C.

JAFFRELOT C. [2005a] (ed.), L'Inde contemporaine : de 1950 à nos jours, 2è edition, Paris: Fayard, 1997. 742 p.

JAFFRELOT C. [2005b], Inde, la démocratie par la caste, histoire d'une mutation socio-politique, Fayard, Paris.

JALAN B. [2005], The Future of India, Politics, Economics and Governance, Viking-Penguin New Delhi.

MADDISON A. [2003], The World Economy, Historical Statistics, OECD, Paris.

MARIA A. [2004], Remaking India, One country, One Destiny, Response Books, New Delhi.

MARKOVITS C. [1994], Histoire de l'Inde moderne : 1480-1950, Paris, Ed. Fayard.

McKinsey & Company [2005], "The Emerging Global Labour Market: Part I - The Demand for Offshore Talent in Services", June 2005.

NASSCOM [2005], Handbook for ITES-BPO Industry 2005, New Delhi June 2005, http://www.nasscom.org/

PLANNING COMMISSION [2002a], Employment Generating Growth, report of the special group on "Targeting ten million employment opportunities per year", New Delhi.

PLANNING COMMISSION [2002b], Report of the Committee on India Vision 2020, Government of India, New Delhi.

PNUD [2004], Human Development Report, Geneva.

RAMESH J. [2005], Making Sense of Chindia, India Research Press, New Delhi.

RIS [2004], South Asia Development and Cooperation Report 2004.

RODRIK D., SUBRAMANIAN A. [2004a], «From "Hindu Growth" to Productivity Surge: The Mystery of the Indian Growth Transition», NBER Working Paper 10376.

RODRIK D., SUBRAMANIAN A. [2004b], «Why India Can Grow at 7 Percent a Year or More: Projections and Reflections», IMF Working Paper WP/04/118.

RUET Joël [2005], Réformes et modèles de développement en Inde, Futuribles juillet-août 2005, numéro 310.

SADHANA S. [2003], "What is the True Level of FDI Flows to India?", Economic and Political Weekly 15 Février 2003, Mumbai.

SEN A. [1999], Development as Freedom, First Anchor Books Edition.

SEN A., DREZE J. [2002], India's Economic Development and Participation, Oxford University Press, New Delhi.

TERI [2002], Green India 2047, Directions, Innovations, and Strategies for Harnessing Action for Sustainable Development, revised edition, New Delhi.

UNCTAD [2004], World Investment Report, Geneva.

United Nations (2005), World Population Prospects, The 2004 Revision, Department of Economic and Social Affairs, Population Division, New York.

VIRMANI A. [2004a], "India's Economic Growth: From Socialist Rate of Growth to Bharatiya Rate of Growth".

ICRIER Working Paper No. 122, New Delhi.

VIRMANI A. [2004b], "Economic Performance, Power Potential and Global Governance: Towards a New International Order", ICRIER Working Paper No. 150.

WILLIAMSON J., ZAGHA R. [2002], "From the Hindu Rate of Growth to the Hindu Rate of Reform", Working Paper.

No. 144, Centre for Research on Economic Development and Policy Reform, Stanford University, USA, July, 2002.

World Bank [2005], World Development Indicators, Washington D.C., The World Bank Group.

ZINS Max-Jean : Histoire politique de l'Inde indépendante, PUF, Paris, 1992, 336 p.

Index

Q

R

S

T